Levinson Travel

Italy's Best with Kids

MAX PUBLICATIONS, INC,
Atlanta, Georgia

To David, I love you more today than yesterday,
but not half as much as tomorrow.
Debra

———————————

Copyright © 2004 by Max Publications, Inc.

Book design: Jill Dible
Edited by: Rhonda Hill
Cover design and graphics: Gabe Liner
Creative consultant: Susan Heller Shoer
Photography: A special thanks to our sons Ari, Isaac and
Jacob Levinson for their numerous artistic contributions
Proofreading: Erika Buchkowski and Jacob Levinson
Property reviews: Debra Levinson

ORDER MORE COPIES:

IN YOUR LOCAL BOOK STORES or
VISIT US ON LINE AT: www.levinsontravel.com

Levinson Travel Guides
Max Publications, Inc.
825 Malvern Hill • Alpharetta, Georgia 30022
USA: Telephone: 800-255-0623 / 770-664-0825 / 770-851-0935
Fax: 770-740-0188
Outside USA: Telephone: ++ 001-770-664-0825
Fax: ++ 001-770-740-0188

Cover images: Top of Italy's Map going downward: Jacob, Isaac, and Ari Levinson riding their **Patmont Motor Werks** Go-Ped's around the *Roman Colosseum;* Drs. Debra and David Levinson; Central Italy's Residence *Il Pozzetto* near the town of Anghiari; Isaac Levinson hiking central Italy's Cinque Terre on the Ligurian Coast; Hotel Villa Belvedere in Taormina, Sicily; Sardinia: Jacob, Isaac, and Ari Levinson

Printed in the United States of America by BookMasters, Inc., Mansfield, Ohio
ISBN: 0-9633577-4-3

DISCLAIMER
The special places to stay are based on our pure subjectivity. This book is an account of our personal opinions and tastes; therefore, we make no claims to our judgments.
We do hope you will share in our sentiments.

We have done our best to ensure that our facts are correct but apologize for any errors that we may have inadvertently missed. From time to time, changes occur and prices fluctuate, so we would appreciate being told of any inaccuracies or changes.

Grazie, The Levinson family

Table of Contents

Northern Italy

Central Italy

Southern Italy

Boats, Skiing, Villas & More

❧ *Foreword* ❧

FAMILY TRAVEL
Our Approach

The key to successful family travel is to operate as partners. Debra and I seem to do so naturally. If one of us is down, the other one is there to be positive. If one is sad, the other is ready to laugh. The key to our success and happiness is that we stop to listen to each other so that we make the decisions that are best for ourselves and for our family.

So it was when we finally arrived at our vacation villa in the foothills of Tuscany. This was to be our home for the next month where we would explore Italy. Our kids would play with local kids, we would shop the markets, and cook authentic Italian meals. Our goal was to immerse ourselves in the Italian culture and countryside, discovering the wonders of nature and the history of this region.

The villa was advertised as being on Lake Trasimeno. It was supposed to be a restored stone villa in a small village, furnished comfortably in antiques. I knew we were in trouble when the house was nowhere near the lake. Furthermore, only if we opened the upstairs bedroom window, stuck out our heads, angled a mirror attached to a stick, then the lake was visible. The furnishings weren't antiques; on the contrary, they were just old. The place was dark and cold, even though it was a warm and sunny day. We were all so tired and terribly disappointed, but we were prepared to make the best of a bad situation. At least one of us was, but the others wouldn't hear of it.

We had to drive a couple of miles to a small hotel just to find a telephone. It was there that we were able to get some help. The owner of the hotel spoke a little English but was nice enough to help us get in touch with the woman in England from whom we rented the villa. We explained to her that the accommodations didn't meet our expectations, nor were they accurately described in her advertisement. We asked her to return our $1,000 deposit. We were ready to move on, yet she wouldn't hear of it and, the more we spoke, the less English she admitted to understanding. Finally, she claimed that not only was she refusing to return our deposit, she also wanted the remainder of the rent for the next three weeks. Despite her refusal to refund our deposit, we were determined not to allow our trip to be ruined.

So out came the map, and we plotted our course to Cortona. It was now early afternoon and the kids were actually doing great. Even though they had to be tired from the trip, they were getting along well and were excited to move on. You would think that we all would have been angry and negative, but we weren't. We all took on the feeling that we were explorers and that we were about to discover something fun and great. At this point, you could say that a transformation took place in all of us. The plan was not to have a plan, and the theme of this vacation was to go in the direction the wind was blowing. By doing this, we would have no expectations and, therefore, no more disappointments. Our goal was to search out fun and interesting places. We would handle our basic needs that, at the time, meant finding a clean and comfortable place to sleep. From there, we would then look for the next adventure.

The car ride to Cortona was actually a lot of fun. It took us only about ninety minutes. We stopped a couple of times and bought some fruit from roadside stands. The countryside was beautiful with the eye-appealing acres of sunflowers and rolling hills. Before we knew it, we could see Cortona sitting high on the mountain. For the kids, it was the first time they had seen a medieval city. The massive walls that surround the city and protect it from long ago threats of invasion appeared exactly like I envisioned it must have looked six hundred years ago. We felt as if we were back in time, traveling through a different land and about to enter the gates of a distant civilization. Our hope was that inside those walls we'd find the hospitality, comfort, and experiences that would make the trip something we would remember for a lifetime.

At the top of the winding road leading to the entrance of Cortona, we stopped and parked the car in the oval parking entrance to the city. There is a fabulous view of villas, farms, and church steeples from inside the city looking over the valley below, and you can see for miles. As you enter the town of Cortona, it is best to travel by foot. The road is narrow and one-way while the cobblestone street is only about fifteen feet wide. On each side of the road are small cafes, markets, boutiques, and antique shops. It was difficult to walk by them without venturing inside. The streets were packed with people: college students hanging out, couples drinking espresso, and kids kicking soccer balls. Some women were walking carrying bags of groceries. The pastry shops beckoned us. The antique shops looked like museums. We were home.

In our quest for accommodations, we decided to split up and check out the hotels in Cortona. There are only about ten hotels, so it doesn't take much time to find a place. After being turned away from most, the Hotel Oasi Neumann was recommended to us (Central Italy). We were told this hotel was a little larger and that there were available rooms. It was about 500 meters outside of town and, because it was just down the hill, it only took about ten minutes to reach. As soon as we arrived, we got the sense that this is a special place and may be the best kept secret in Cortona.

The property sits on the side of the mountain with a great view of the valley. Upon arriving at Hotel Oasi Neumann, we were greeted at the reception desk by a young, handsome man named Stefano. The first thing that struck us was that he was wearing a cervical collar. Stefano's English was excellent, making it easy to explain to him that we were chiropractors and that we would like to help him. Immediately, Stefano showed us to a grand room overlooking the Tuscan valley with large, nearly floor-to-ceiling windows that opened from many directions to beautiful vistas.

We settled in and called for Stefano to come up for his first chiropractic adjustment. We discovered that he had been in a traumatic car accident and had been seeing an orthopedic surgeon who prescribed the collar and muscle relaxers over the past two weeks. At this point, Stefano was no better. I did an exam and performed a chiropractic adjustment. Stefano stood up declaring with joy and enthusiasm that he was pain free. Overcome by his experience, he shared with us that his wedding was in six days and invited us to it. He was so pleased that he would wear the traditional tuxedo rather than a cervical collar.

What an opportunity to go to an Italian wedding in Italy. We imagined platefuls of intricately designed raviolis, lasagna, meats, pastries, cakes, and espresso. This was an occasion that we couldn't pass up. In the days leading up to the wedding, Stefano continued his chiropractic adjustments and brought with him what seemed like the entire population of Cortona. We met and adjusted his fiancée Frederica, his mother, father, other friends and relatives at both the Hotel Oasi Neumann and at their soon-to-be new home in the valley below. Stefano also set up a room in the hotel where I would work on other people. Father Angelo, owner of Oasi at the time, was one of the first. He came equipped with x-rays of his feet that were causing him much pain. After his first adjustment, he too was delighted. He insisted that we be his guest for dinner at the hotel the next evening, so we accepted this gracious invitation.

We arrived for dinner anticipating a quiet meal for our family and instead we received a royal reception by the entire hotel staff. Apparently the boys had informed them that it was their Mom's birthday. Flowers were presented to Debra as we were seated in a private area of the restaurant, joined by Father Angelo, Stefano, and Frederica. The Tuscan feast was incredible, topped off by a freshly made birthday cake and "Happy Birthday" sung in Italian as we toasted our new friends.

Getting to the wedding was an adventure in itself. The directions that I had written a few days earlier made little sense…"Turn at the farmhouse with the sunflowers or bear right at the stonewall…" We were undeniably lost. Fortunately Italian weddings extend well into the next day. An older man and his wife directed us up a dirt road that didn't look remotely familiar from the previous day. One last stop for reassurance at an *Agriturismo* (farm holiday), where our route was discussed among a group of people in multiple languages and, two hours later, we were there!

It was well worth the journey. We feasted on an array of homemade *antipasti* (appetizers), meat, pasta salad, fish, fruit, bread, cheese, desserts, wine, and *espresso*; furthermore, an entire pig was displayed and served as well. During the wedding, Stefano even set up a makeshift chiropractic clinic. The line of patients was unending. We noticed that Stefano was collecting *lire* (currency/now called *euro*) although we insisted it wasn't necessary. We finally agreed that any earnings would go to the kids.

The next morning, we headed for the Isle of Elba where the boys decided to use their earnings to rent a motorboat. We relaxed, sun-bathed, and explored reefs. Anchored for lunch on a small alcove beach, we reflected upon the extraordinary occurrences of the past week, recognizing that life holds no coincidences. We learned from this experience the importance of living in the moment. In the course of life, situations don't always turn out as anticipated. We recognize that each day holds the opportunity to recreate our lives and make new choices. Incorporating a flexible attitude together with an optimistic approach is sure to be a winning formula whether traveling down the road of life or through the Tuscan countryside.

As a result of these turns of events we recognized the need for more reliable and better-quality family travel guidebooks. We hope that these stories and memories from our journeys will inspire you to travel to Italy with your family. Please read on for all the information you need to get going.

Buon Viaggio (Have a good trip)!
David Levinson

Debra, David, Isaac, Ari & Jacob Levinson
Villa Meligunis Hotel, Lipari-Isole Eolie (Sicily)

❧ *Introduction* ❧

Most parents want to expose their children to as many sights, sounds, and experiences as possible. Visiting museums, theme parks, and taking road trips are all wonderful ways to be together and create memories; however, mention taking the kids to a place like Italy and these same involved and motivated parents hesitate. Their first thought is of their children's behavior, complete with images of temper tantrums in such a place as Rome's Trevi Fountain. We've spoken to dozens of families who have traveled to Italy with their kids as well as those contemplating the journey, and they all comment on the fact that our boys look forward to our many trips to Italy. We, the Levinson family, are here to describe to you that family travel to Italy can be an incredibly rewarding experience for both parents and kids.

Italy's Best with Kids can be enjoyed both as an informative travel guide complete with full color pictures and detailed amenities as well as fun arm chair reading, taking you behind the scenes into our lives and those people we have met along the way. As we discovered in planning dozens of journeys to Italy with our three boys, a little information and a little preparation go a long way. Creating the right itineraries, staying in the right places, and choosing the correct age appropriate activities will hold the interest of children enough for their parents to also enjoy the trip. These same parents have asked us, "Are *my* children old enough to appreciate Italy?" Our answer, regardless of age, is always, "Yes!". Now, does your seven-year-old have to appreciate the Sistine Chapel, the mountains of Carrara, the fine cuisine of a quaint trattoria, or the historic beauty of an old cathedral? No, of course not. Most kids will no more want to spend an entire day searching for antiques than you would want to spend an entire day in a video game arcade! Even two adults can have very different ideas of what is fun to see and do.

David and I met in 1978 while attending a chiropractic college in Atlanta, Georgia. From the start, a tradition began. To celebrate our birthdays, we would surprise each other with an extended weekend trip. We secretly planned each detail and packed each other's bags. Twice a year soon became four to six times a year, while long weekends eventually turned into a week. Once we graduated from the chiropractic college, our friends were sure these jaunts would end. Certainly, we would be too busy starting our practice; however, we proved friends wrong as our lust for travel and adventure continued. In fact, we discovered that time away was an opportunity to reevaluate our relationship both at home and work. Our minds were cleared, our hearts opened to give, and our love to serve people was in greater capacity. Monday mornings back at the practice consistently brought an increase in new patients and additional revenue. Many of our colleagues who observed this phenomenon followed suit, yet others just couldn't break away from the hectic pace of the workplace.

After five years of marriage and practice, our first child Jacob was born. Again we were subjected to hearing, "Now that you have a baby, you won't be able to travel like you used to." At six weeks old, Jake was on his first plane flight and excursion. Our second son Isaac was only four weeks old before we were off and flying while our youngest son Ari began traveling at a mere three weeks of age. Initially, the trips weren't the type of romantic interludes to which we were accustomed but, in time and through trial and error, we developed a way to create fun for the kids yet craft time for ourselves.

Jacob is now sixteen years old and, as a result of his exposure to other cultures through travel, he desired the opportunity to be placed in an educational environment that would satisfy his thirst to learn other languages. He has been attending an international school in Atlanta where the student body is comprised of sixty-four nationalities. This has given him the type of immersion he was looking for and, as a result of his education, he's fluent in French, Spanish, and Italian.

Isaac, at thirteen years old, exudes a different spirit and drive. Viewing the Tour-de-France cycling course through the Alps, snowboarding the Dolomite Mountains, and being exposed to some of the greatest chefs of the world, has given him a vision that what the mind can conceive and believe it will achieve. He attends a school in Atlanta that affords him time to pursue his appreciation for cooking and extreme sports training.

Ari is ten years old and attends a school in Atlanta with an emphasis on academics accompanied by an importance on self-expression that makes this an ideal environment for him. The world is a stage for Ari, and he looks for every possible opportunity to perform. Hearing a violin echoing from an apartment window above a narrow *strada* (street), an unanticipated Shakespearean play in a medieval *piazza* (town center), and the drama of everyday life in Rome has shown him that the stage is an expression of life.

We invite you to leave the hectic pace of life behind, dispense of your preconceived notions of traveling with kids, and join us for the journey of a lifetime. We have designed a simple format to help guide you to the perfect vacation spots for your family. A great place to start is the chapter on *Highlights of the Regions*, select the area you would most like to explore, and then turn to the corresponding segment of places to stay and decide on the accommodation that appeals most to your family. These extraordinary properties are located throughout Italy and are divided into three sections: Northern, Central, and Southern Italy, with a special section inclusive of villa rentals, boating excursions, winter ski holidays, and summer camps. Each section combines several regions of Italy. Involve your children in the decisions by allowing their input when making travel plans. We have provided websites to further acquaint you with all of our *Italy's Best with Kids* properties and excursions, along with telephone, fax, and e-mail addresses. All of our property owners and managers will welcome your correspondence. Identify yourself as learning about the properties from this publication, and the property owners will recognize the benefit of being featured in this guide and may offer you a special rate.

What's our secret for unforgettable family vacations in Italy? First, we begin each day with an activity that centers on the kids doing what they enjoy. We've discovered the best way to ensure everyone's happiness is to create fun each day with a focus on the kids. Before you take a drive shopping for linen or visiting medieval cities, it's essential to give the kids an opportunity for physical activity. Otherwise, you will end up with a stiff neck, constantly turning around to break up the tension and the frustration in the back seat of the car.

For our boys, being in or on water is their favorite activity. So, whenever possible, we try to stay near a lake, a beach, a pool, or a water-park within a ten minute drive. David is a master at turning an ordinary event into a game so that we can do what we love and enjoy while the boys are totally engrossed in the same activity with a slightly different twist. For example, on our first trip with the boys to the Cinque Terre, in the Liguria region, we were determined to walk the entire coastal route, about 12 *kilometers*. How do we convince Ari, at six years old, that not only is he capable of making the walk but that it will be fun? The answer? *Gelato* (ice cream).

The Cinque Terre consists of five towns connected by a footpath, and David promised the boys that in each town they would be rewarded with gelato, first with one scoop, then two scoops, followed by three, four, and five helpings if they made it to each town. We took our time and enjoyed the flavors of gelato at each stop, in addition to sampling *focaccia al formaggio* (pizza bread), a bowl of pasta with *pesto* (basil sauce) and truly some of the best food the region has to offer, broken up with an occasional swim in the Mediterranean. In fact, once our children were mature enough, we felt comfortable allowing them to go off on their own while visiting some of Italy's small rural cities. We would give them a small amount of Euros to buy some *gelato* or a small souvenir. This gave the kids a sense of independence while giving us some time alone to pursue an activity that was of interest to us.

Visiting the Cinque Terre with children was very different from how David and I approached the Cinque Terre on a previous visit without kids. The two of us hiked at a quicker pace with fewer stops. In fact, we walked there and back in the same day. Seeing it the child-friendly way certainly gave us a different perspective.

Where do you begin in your quest to plan the perfect family vacation? This is the question we faced when first starting to plan family trips to Italy. We found many general information books about Italy with their primary focus centered on Rome, Venice, Verona, Florence, Pisa, and Milan. These are all beautiful and valuable places to see, but we were also interested in finding some private and out-of-the-way places that we would find intriguing and romantic as well as those the kids would find exciting and fun-filled.

Italy's Best with Kids travel guidebook is our latest family endeavor. We want to give family travelers an appreciation for the roads less traveled in Italy along with enough information to create their own special journeys. Those with an adventurous spirit who choose not to settle for the mundane in life will benefit from our experiences. Whether your family members are seasoned travelers or first time adventure seekers, the magic of Italy will unfold within these pages.

We also want to share all the discoveries we've made over the past six years about accommodations that are close to the most intriguing sites near wildlife preserves, mountains, rivers, and seas. Most of the properties we have included in the following pages are historic and provide an opportunity for kids to appreciate the country's multi-layered culture. We've identified locations that can be your home base for seeing several different areas. As you will discover, part of the joys when traveling with children is to stay in one ideal place for several consecutive nights in order to avoid repeated packing and unpacking.

You can truly vacation with kids and have every experience you've ever imagined, whether it be snowboarding and skiing the Italian Alps, climbing the spectacular Dolomite mountain ranges, or even soaking in the ancient Roman and Etruscan mineral baths. You can unwind by cruising down the Veneto region's Brenta Canal or Venice's labyrinth-like waterways for an independent boating holiday. We've created a one-stop guide that will tell you everything you need to know about Italy's sports and recreational activities and historic properties.

Our family has vacationed at and reviewed each property and we've personally experienced every ski and boat trip. We have identified the most family-oriented hotels, inns, resorts, and villas throughout most Italian regions; furthermore, all are selected for their quality of family friendliness, charm, food, housekeeping, proximity to sightseeing, recreation, and sporting activities as well as appropriateness for children.

A visit to Italy is always memorable and meaningful. Seeing Italy through your children's eyes is a gift. Children live in the moment, and they will often inspire you to do the same. We hope that this book will help you create the family vacation of a lifetime. *La dolce vita* is waiting for all of you!

Goda fare le memorie insieme,
(Enjoy making memories together)
Debra Levinson

✍ Kids Perspective ✍

JACOB'S ACCOUNT: As the oldest of three boys, and at age sixteen, I sometimes get to experience special activities that my brothers aren't old enough to do. When we first started going to Italy, I was able to see things a little differently from them. I remember the first time we arrived in Rome, and our plan was to drive straight to Hotel Adriano Ristorante (Central Italy) after the long flight. As soon as we set our eyes on the *Colosseum*, we immediately abandoned that practical and sensible idea of first checking in. My parents instantaneously found a parking spot next to the Roman *Colosseum*, which was a feat in itself. As we began walking towards this historic edifice, our jet lag seemed to melt away. Considering it stands over 160 ft high with eighty entrances, and is large enough to hold more then 50,000 spectators energized me. Furthermore, having prior knowledge that public events such as gladiator fights, mock naval battles and wild animal hunts were held at the *Colosseum* hastened my pace.

Walking along the ancient cobblestone pathway leading into the *Colosseum*, I was overcome by a strange feeling. I said to my Mom, "I've been here before." My Mom told me I was an old soul. It's funny, but there are certain times and places in Italy that make our family feel that we've previously been here, even though we never have.

Nowadays, the Roman *Colosseum* is one of Italy's best known landmarks and tourist attractions. In my studies at the International School I took a course that emphasized building structure along with design. I now see the *Colosseum* not only as a historic ruin but one of the finest examples of Roman architecture and engineering. Familiarize your kids through books, videos, and the Internet beforehand; it will add color and interest to what they're seeing.

Goda (Enjoy)
Jacob Levinson

ISAAC'S SUGGESTIONS: Hi, my name is Isaac. I'm thirteen, and the middle child. Through the years, my brothers and I have developed a list of items to take with us on the airplane. We each have a backpack, which has proven useful to keep our things organized throughout the trip. Your kids will have their own interests, but here are some ideas to get you started: GameBoy, CD player, extra batteries, laptop and movies, DVD's, books, playing cards, small travel games and toys (Milton Bradley makes miniature Monopoly, Trouble, etc.), snack foods, toiletries, and a wash cloth. Each of us packs a change of clothes just in case we spill something or our luggage doesn't make it to our destination. I like to bring a pair of swim shoes, which makes it easier to slip on and go to the bathroom. If you are in business class, many of these things will be given to you.

In addition to the items for the plane, we each take disposable cameras, a photo album or scrapbook, walkie-talkies with a two-mile range, sunglasses, and hats. My mom always travels with a first-aid kit of natural homeopathic remedies, teas, and additional food.

Each time we check into a different hotel, we put their business card in our pack, and we carry one with us in case of an emergency. My brothers and I have enjoyed taking our scooters and go-peds. The gas can needs to be clean of any fuel. Box them up and send as baggage. They are great to zip through towns when my parents take their time in antique shops or sit and drink cappuccinos. When we have traveled with other families who have babies and small kids, the backpacks designed to carry them in are great.

Have fun, and enjoy making memories together!

Ciao,
Isaac Levinson

ARI'S STORY: My name is Ari, I am ten, and I'm the youngest in the family. You might wonder how we started traveling to Italy. My Mom got so tired of staying in Georgia day in and day out, driving us to school every day, that she decided to take my dad, David, on an adventure somewhere no one had been before to a little place called Italy. They packed their bags and left the next week.

Two weeks later, they came back with so many great stories that my two brothers and I got really excited about seeing Italy ourselves. One month later we were on our way. We went to the Cinque Terre, Rome, Venice, and many other great places. After we got home from our first trip, we decided it was so much fun that we should go every summer, and we have ever since.

I have some advice for the kids in the family. First, there are a few Italian words you need to know such as: *dov'è il bagno,* which is "where is the bathroom," or *mi scusi,* which is "excuse me," *grazie*, which is "thank you," and *ciao* or *arrivederci,* which is "goodbye." Make sure your parents let you eat lots of this great Italian ice cream called *gelato*. My favorite flavors are *limone,* which is lemon, *fragola,* which is strawberry, *melone,* which is melon, and *cioccolata,* which is chocolate.

When you go to Italy, you will see lots and lots of sunflowers that are more than five feet tall. These flowers are so pretty you will want to take hundreds of pictures of them. At least I did. My family would love to hear about your family adventures in Italy. So if you can e-mail us about your discoveries and adventures, we could put your story in our next version of this book. You can send them to postmaster@levinsontravel.com.

Buon divertimento!
(Have fun!)
Ari Levinson

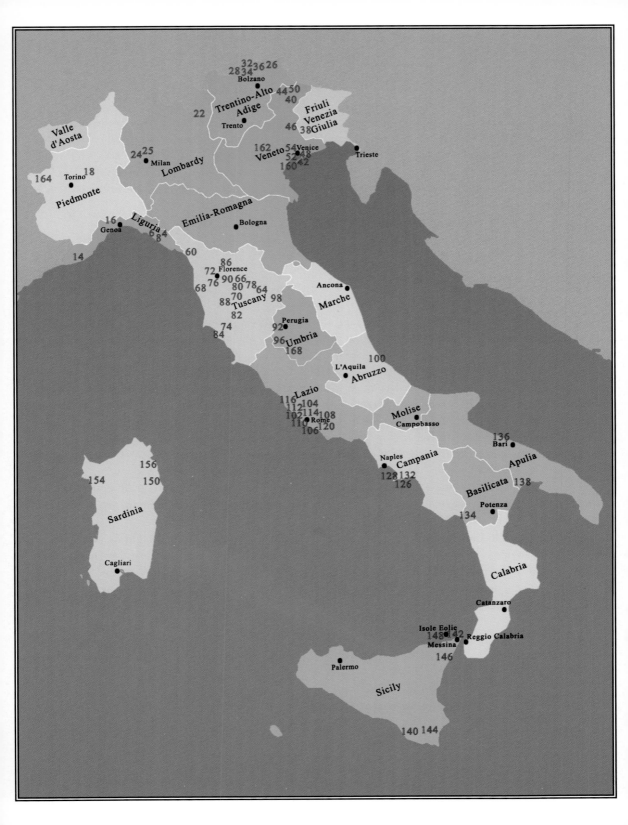

Valle d'Aosta

Piedmonte

164
Torino 18

Lombardy
24 25
Milan

Trentino-Alto Adige
Bolzano
28 32 36 26
34
22
Trento
44 50
40

Friuli Venezia Giulia
46 38

Veneto
162 54 Venice
52 48
160 42

Trieste

Liguria
16
Genoa
64
68
14

Emilia-Romagna
Bologna

60

Tuscany
86
72 Florence
90 66
76 80 78 64
68 70
88 82
74
84
98

Marche
Ancona

Umbria
Perugia
92
96
168

Abruzzo
L'Aquila
100

Lazio
116 104
112 114
102 108
110 120
Rome
106

Molise
Campobasso

Campania
Naples
128 132
126

Apulia
136
Bari
138

Basilicata
Potenza
134

Sardinia
156
154 150

Cagliari

Calabria

Catanzaro

Isole Eolie
148 142
Messina
146
Reggio Calabria

Palermo

Sicily

140 144

◈ *Highlights of the Regions* ◈

Along with special places of interest to see, each geographic region brings its own personality to the richness of the foods and wines themselves. In this segment of *Italy's Best with Kids* we have accentuated some of the most important features the regions have to offer regarding what to see, eat, and drink. This is only a slight representation of the vastness yet to discover. Previous knowledge of these aspects during your trip-planning phase will give you a clearer sense of where and how you would like to spend your time in Italy. Allow yourself to be guided by your curiosity through the suggestions we have made. Venture confidently knowing that a wrong turn may perhaps lead to your own secret treasure. Once you have selected the regions that most attract your interests, turn to the corresponding accommodation section and select the *Italy's Best* property that ideally suits your family's desires. The price guides that accompany each accommodation review are intended as a range, giving you an approximation of cost comparison from one property to another. Most hotels usually list price as a per person rate. Utilizing our *Reservation Request Form* will provide you with personalized information according to your specific needs.

NORTHERN ITALY

Valle d'Aosta: This region lies in the northwest corner of Italy in the heart of the Alps; it borders with Switzerland, France, and the region of Piemonte. Aosta is the best town to explore the different valleys with their great hiking and skiing opportunities. Ski trails abound in this small region, as well as three world-class winter resorts: Cervinia, Champoluc and Courmayeur, the latter of which is considered one of the most elegant in Italy connecting to Chamonix in France by a road tunnel and a cable car climbing to over 3,800 m. Valtournenche, while boasting the famous Matterhorn, is an important ski resort as well as one of the greatest sightseeing areas in the Aosta Valley. At the northwestern end of the Val d'Aosta you find Mont Blanc, the highest peak in Europe. For one of the greatest thrills, journey by cable car ride over Mont Blanc into France. This region is an absolute gold mine for feudal castles and towers from the middle ages, particularly along the Dora Baltea River. The mountain resort of Saint-Vincent is a great starting point for touring the many castles of Valle d'Aosta, in addition to Europe's largest casino, mineral water spas, inspiring mountain hikes, and Italy's oldest park, Gran Paradiso National Park. The Lys valley protects its characteristic alpine appearance and has two main resorts: Gressoney-St-Jean and Gressoney-La-Trinité. Mount Rosa, a huge glacier covered massif with ten summits separates the Lys from the Ayas valley, where the main sights of interest are Brusson, Champoluc, Antagnod and Saint Jacques. The foods are rich in dairy products and definitely designed for heating you up in cold, mountain weather, including roasted meats, cheese and mushrooms. *Fontina* cheese is the best known cheese of the region. The Northern Italian version of cheese fondue is a *fonduta,* made with fontina cheese melted with milk, eggs, and flour. The area's best wines are primarily local varieties of reds and whites ranging from their own Donnaz and Enfer d'Arvier, as well as the white wines of Morgex and La Salle, Piedmonte's Nebbiolo, Dolcetto, and Moscato to the French Pinots and Gamay.

Piedmonte: This is an appealing region with some French influences, delightful food, and superb wines. There are lots of places to hike and bike in this region. Piedmont's portion of the Italian lakes includes Lake Orta and the whole western half of Lake Maggiore, joining together beautiful nature and inspiring art. Turin, the capital of Piemonte, is a fascinating European city with an international quality and home to the much-disputed reproduction of the Holy Shroud that Jesus was allegedly wrapped in after he was removed from the cross, on view in the cathedral of San Giovanni. In Turin you will also find a most important museum of Egyptian artifacts existing outside of Egypt, the Automotive Museum, and the Savoy's Royal Palace. Stresa, previously a small fishing village, has developed into a popular tourist area located on one of the most attractive parts of Lake Maggiore. Castles are plentiful as are the region's highly prized and very costly white truffles that grow underground beneath certain oak trees. Food connoisseurs come from all over Italy and the world every fall to gather these unusual items, bringing them to the world's finest restaurants and into special products such as truffle-scented olive oil. Truffles are also used to enhance pastas, risottos, meats, and cheeses. The area is home to a large collection of full-bodied red wines, including Bardo and Barbaresco and to one of the foremost sparkling wines of the world, Asti Spumante.

Liguria: The southern half of Liguria's coast, the Riviera di Ponente, extends from France to Genoa, Italy. It encompasses such beautiful turn-of-the-century resort towns as San Remo and Finale Liqure. The lustrous Riviera di Levante, the coast from Genoa to La Spezia, is one of Italy's most famous. It consists of a multitude of charming fishing villages, the best known of which is Portofino. A stay on the Ligurian cost is incomplete without a visit to the Cinque Terre's five scenic fishing villages. Each of the towns has something different to offer and it's a must to see them all. One of the best ways to see the Cinque Terre is to hike the many trails that join them, or the train that runs between them. Genoa has many sites to see including Christopher Columbus's home, the 12th century cloisters of Sant'Andrea, and the Royal Palace, which contains an excellent collection of European art works. This bounteous agricultural land along the coast offers many culinary riches. Ligurians have a deep affection for their traditional *pesto* sauce with its main ingredients being fresh basil, pine nuts, garlic, and *Parmigiano Reggiano* or *Pecorino cheese*. Olive oil and wine are chief products, as well as sweet chestnuts and their esteemed porcino mushrooms that grow beneath the tree. Coastally, seafood is plentiful, but traveling inland through Liquria features poultry and duck. Complete your gastronomic journey with the rich tasting *digestive liqueur* of *Limoncello*. This region has produced a very small but flavorful group of red and white wines. One of the most outstanding is the Cinqueterre, a white wine made around the five-terraced fishing villages nestled in the cliffs along the coast.

Lombardy: Milan, the largest city in Lombardy, is a big-commerce city with hundreds of banks and corporate offices, blending old and new. The city also has many points of interest including the Duomo, impressive cathedrals, incredible designer shopping and boutiques, La Scala (a world-renowned opera house), Leonardo's masterpiece, the "Last Supper," and the enchanting navigli whose canals border some of Italy's trendiest restaurants. Lake Como is a favorite vacation spot for Europeans that combines gorgeous scenery and fine art, with invigorating mountain air. Take a relaxing boat trip to the many noble villas and gardens or to the charming villages of Bellagio, Tremezzo, Varenna. Piazza Cavour in the town of Lake Como has lakeside cafes and fashionable shopping boutiques, with breathtaking views of the snow-capped Alps. Nearby is Lake Maggiore with its three islands: Isola Bella, Isola dei Pescatori, and Isola Madre. Three other Lombardy towns deserving a visit are Bergamo with its

Piazza Vecchia, considered one of the most picturesque squares in all of Italy; Mantova's Ducal Palace, with its series of frescoes by Mantegna;, and Cremona, famous for the art of making stringed instruments by Stradivari. The golf courses in this region are among the most beautiful. Lombardy has very diverse dietary and gastronomic habits throughout the various cities. Olive oil, remarkable cheeses, rice, and fresh cured meats are abundant throughout the region. Milan, in particular, seems to be a freethinking city and consequently more inclined to contemporaneous cuisine in which specialties from different Italian regions are included with local dishes. These local dishes are typified by risotto with saffron, minestrone with a range of variations, *cassoeula* (pork and savoy cabbage stew), *costoletta* (flattened, breaded and fried veal chop), *busecca* (a tripe and giblet soup), *ossobuco* (braised veal shank with the marrow bone) and *Panettone*, the traditional Christmas cake. The primary grapes used for sparkling white wines include Chardonnay, Pinot Bianco, Pinot Grigio, and Pinot Nero. Rosés, and various reds such as Cabernet, Merlot and Rosato are readily available.

Trentino-Alto Adige: This area along Italy's northeastern border of Austria is a spectacular land of jagged ridges and snow-capped peaks, luminous waterfalls and sweeping meadows, and fabulous ski resorts with enchanting medieval towns. In winter, the skiing is absolutely first rate. Spring and fall offer captivating hikes and climbs along a wide-ranging series of well-marked trails, with stops in distant mountain hamlets. Castles abound throughout Trentino Alto Adige, and many are open to visitors; some have even been transformed into hotels or restaurants. For lovers of culture and history, this area has much to offer: the provinces of Trento or Bozen (both provinces with their own individual autonomy) have numerous historic sites, museums, and important monuments. This has been a politically divided region since Mussolini placed it under the realm of the Austrian Habsburgs and then returned it to Italy at the end of World War I; therefore, many of the localities have had two names. Bozen/Bolzano is a city where Italian and German cultures flawlessly blend together. On view at South Tyrol's Museum of Archaeology is the five thousand year old "Iceman" discovered in 1991. Brixen/Bressanone is the main town of the valley, which exudes artistic and historical riches as well as a special charm. The Plose Mountain soars over the town and is an eminent ski resort. Meran/Merano contains famous parks and gardens, promenades, and footpaths in addition to its medieval town center. Trento/Trentino stands as a crossroad for the diverse cultures of Italy and Northern Europe. Visit the Castello del Buonconsiglio, the castle that was home to the prince bishops of Trento for many centuries and the *Duomo* (cathedral) with its splendid square. The food of Trentino Alto Adige has a German influence and the fundamental components are *polenta* (corn meal) prepared in various ways and smoked meat, particularly local *speck*, boneless pork meat cut in small square pieces and placed in saltpeter with garlic, laurel, juniper, pepper, and other herbs. Mushrooms are plentiful and are used to make luscious sauces served with polenta and pasta, and particular meat dishes. Vegetables are primarily beets, cabbage, potatoes, and turnips. The regions' apples are full of flavor making their traditional strudels and *zelten* (tartlet of dried fruit and nuts) irresistible. Wine choices are plentiful: Riesling, Sauvignon, golden Muskateller, Chardonnay, and many sparkling white wines are balanced with a smaller but equally flavorful group of Cabernets and Merlots.

Veneto: This area is a hidden treasure and one relatively unpopulated with tourists. Most people associate this region with Venice, a fascinating city of labyrinth like canals, alleyways, charming homes, notable villas, and distinguished by impressive squares with stately buildings. The Jewish ghetto of Venice is an extraordinary and unique quarter with five synagogues (15th to 16th century), and ancient pawnshops; however to venture no further would mean missing so many other magnificent places. Verona is one of the most eye-catching and historical cities. It's home to the Capulet house with Juliet's legendary balcony, outstanding Roman ruins, Medieval and Renaissance buildings. The city is full of music and its piazzas and streets are generally festive during the annual summer opera festival held in the Roman Arena. Vicenza is an essential visit for any lover of architecture. Andrea Palladio moved here as a child and without doubt has left his mark all throughout the city of Vicenza. He is known for the fundamental use of column rows and harmonization of his work in accordance with the surrounding land. In Padua one can also appreciate works by Medieval and Renaissance artists, of whom Giotto's frescoes are truly the most important ones. Valpolicella is a fertile valley covered with innumerable family wineries, offering never-ending panoramas and enchanting countryside. Fifteenth century walls surround Treviso, perfectly safeguarding its remarkable architectural and artistic masterpieces. Abano, a thermal spa town located in the center of this region, has hot water springs long recognized since Roman times. Chioggia, a small-Venice with picturesque canals and busy riverbanks is alive with people buying fish and vegetables in the markets. Lake Garda, surrounded by the snowy Alps, is perfect for windsurfing, sailing, and canoeing, as well as for all yachting and fishing. In Marostica you can watch a human chess game whose living pieces are dressed in Renaissance costumes, just as it had occurred back in 1454 when Marostica belonged to the Venetian Republic. Few places are more picturesque than Cortina d`Ampezzo, Europe's classiest ski resorts. The cuisine of Venice is traditionally herb and spice-based ever since the days when European trade in spices was controlled from the city. *Polenta* (corn meal) originated in the Veneto and is traditionally served with peas, meat, or shellfish. Venetian cooks are proud of their ability to combine foods and create sauces to enhance the original flavor of the ingredients. The unusual white asparagus of Bassano prepared in various ways is legendary. Italians have been making an incredible array of cured meats for thousands of years. In the Veneto, pork with the likely addition of chicken livers or veal is most prevalent. The Veneto is one of Italy's top regions in total wine production. Veneto wines consist of a large group of reds and rosés such as Bardolino, Valpolicella, Cabernet Sauvignon, and Cabernet. The sparkling Prosecco's combined with peaches known as a Bellini, is the Veneto's signature drink made famous at Harry's Bar in Venice.

Friuli Venezia Giulia: Friuli is close to Austria, Slovenia, and Croatia in Italy's Northeastern corner. This is not an area that is referred to often in other guidebooks; however, this is a diverse region beaming with beaches, secluded alpine villages, Roman ruins, splendid country villas, snow-capped mountains, rocky seaside cliffs, seaports and picturesque fishing villages. Trieste, the primary sightseeing destination of the area has the Cathedral of S. Giusto with two Romanesque basilicas that were united together in the fourteenth century. If you're interested in archeology the arch of Riccardo (33 B.C.) and the Roman theatre (1st and 2nd centuries A.D.) are inspiring sites. Triste's Giuseppe Verdi theatre hosts their famed opera season in addition to the International Operetta Festival. The Castle of Miramare is a wonderful revision of a medieval castle, extending out into the sea. A park containing English and Italian gardens, unusual plants, sculptures, and ponds surrounds it. In Gorizia, the esteemed Attems Petzenstein Palace houses an art museum and the Museum of the Synagogue, besides housing documentation on the history of the Jewish community, displays paintings of the poet and philosopher Carlo Michelstaedter. The Marano Lagoon is home to countless migrating waterfowl, while Grado is a village composed of narrow streets reminiscent of Venice's smaller canals and pathways. This ancient fishing village is adjacent to a beach resort and well-known health spa. *Polenta* (corn meal) is the food most often found on a table in Friuli accompanied by flavorsome sauces, game, chicken, rabbit or salted cheeses such as *frico* fried in butter. Soups are typically made with beans, greens, or pork ribs, and lots of lard. The weather and time of year influences the availability in the mountains. The woodlands are abundant with mushrooms, herbs, fruit crops, and game. The Trieste and Grado area are influenced by the Venetian manner of preparing seafood with definite Slavic and Austrian flavors. Over three hundred types of wines are produced here, with a wide spread range of rich reds to sparkling white, particularly Bernarda, Tocai, Merlot, Sauvignon, Pinot, Vino del Collio, Picolit, and Verduzzo di Rocca.

CENTRAL ITALY

Emilia-Romagna: Its coastal towns of Rimini and Misano Adriatico are a summertime paradise with miles and miles of sandy beaches. Just about any outdoor activity is readily available, such as deep-sea fishing, hot springs, mud baths and water sports. Additionally, there is a wealth of restaurants, night-clubs, and discotheques. The charming city of Ravenna is situated on the Adriatic halfway between Venice and Florence and is best known for the brilliant mosaic ornamentation of its churches and tombs from its Byzantine past. On the banks of the river Po is the superb renaissance city of Ferrara with its *palazzos* (palaces), shops, cafés, and narrow medieval streets. In San Marino, cars are forbidden in the medieval town. This facilitates the exploration of the city by foot: wander along winding narrow streets lined with red-roofed stone houses, medieval walls, and fortresses. Bologna is the capital and heart of Emilia-Romagna and a region of notable artists such as Carracci, Parmigianini, and the great Pavarotti. Lamborghini and Ferrari sports cars; in addition, Ducati motorcycles are manufactured here. Cobbled streets surround Romanesque and Gothic art, while medieval *palazzos* and majestic towers typify it. *Bologna la grassa* (Bologna the fat) is a title the city has acquired for its rich characteristic food. *Tortellini* is one of its most renowned dishes, stuffed with Parmesan cheese, pork, raw ham, turkey breast egg, and *mortadella* (minced pork meat) from Bologna. Emilia-Romagna is considered a single region from a political perspective, but in actuality it is two separate regions, especially when it comes to its cuisines. Emilia, specifically Parma, is the home of the salamis. It's thought that *prosciutto* (cured ham of Parma) is sweeter than from any other region in Italy. *Culatello di Zibello* (cured leg of an adult hog) is another specialty of the area. Modena preferes the *Zampone and Cotechino di Modena,* which are cured meat products made from a combination of pork taken from striated muscle fibers, pork fat, pigskin, and different seasonings. Romagna's food preparation embraces aromatic herbs and the use of skewers to roast seafood, chicken, game, other meats, and a variety of sausages. There are nearly three hundred types of wines here for every taste. They include Lambrusco, Merlot, Cabernet Sauvignon, Sangiovese, and Barbera for the reds and Albana, Chardonnay, Sauvignon, and Riesling for the whites.

Tuscany: Tuscany, *Toscana* in Italian, is the most well-known Italian region with its many little picturesque hilltop towns, amid vineyards of grape vines and olive trees with gently rolling hillsides, twisting roads, villas, and castles. The most well-known cities such as Florence, Pisa, Lucca, and Siena hold many fascinating attractions to see. Florence produced the greatest works of architecture, sculpture, and paintings by some of the foremost artists of the world: Leonardo da Vinci, Michelangelo

Buonarroti, and Filippo Brunelleschi. Their work, as well as that of many other generations of artists up to the present time, are gathered in the many museums throughout the city. The Uffizi, the most select picture gallery in the world, displays Renaissance art featuring the works of da Vinci, Botticelli, Michaelangelo, Raffaello, Canaletto, and many more. Visit the Rooms of the Planets at the Galleria Palatina. The Galleria dell`Accademia hosts very important painting collections along with well-known works by Michelangelo including *The David*. The collection at Stibbert's museum focuses on the history and traditions of various cultures, and includes weapons, armor, costumes, furnishings, examples of the applied arts with 16th to 19th century tapestries and paintings. Visit the Medici Chapel and the Buonarroti House, with Michaelangelo's sculptures. The Museo degli Argenti or Silver Museum is located in Palazzo Pitti and houses various kinds of precious objects such as gems, cameos, semi-precious stones, ivories, jewels, and silver. The Leaning Tower is of course Pisa's main attraction. Lucca, the birthplace of Giacomo Puccini, is a charming walled city whereas Siena, with its Piazza del Campo, is home to the world-famous Palio horse race. However, venturing outside their municipalities will put you in the heart of some of the most authentic medieval villages and seaside towns: South-East of Florence are Arezzo, Cortona, Montepulciano, and Montalcino; South of Florence and Siena are San Gimignano, Pienza, Pitigliano, Saturnia, Grosseto, and the island of Elba; North-West of Florence, Lucca, and Pisa are Forte dei Marmi, Viareggio, and Carrara. When you think of Italian cuisine and wine, Tuscany definitely comes to mind. The approach to food has always been in its simplicity, based on the love of wine, olive oil, and bread. The bread is never wasted but used as the main ingredient for several common dishes. Most well known are *Panzanella* salad made with bread, tomato, onion, and olive oil as well as *Ribollita*, a thick soup prepared with green vegetables, cabbage, beans and olive oil. Fresh pasta, particularly *parppardella, ravioli, pici, and tordelli* along with the existence of basil, rosemary, sage, parsley, marjoram, bay leaves, and thyme has been part of the *Etruscan* kitchen for centuries. Vegetables combined with fish, beans, and meat grilled over an open fire is regular fare on the Tuscan table. This region has produced table wines recognized as being among the greatest in the world. Chianti is its most notable, while the other reds enable you to feel the warmth and excitement of Tuscany. The most famous variety of grapes is Montepulciano and Sangiovese. The whites are pleasant and enchant the palate.

Marche: This region lies on the eastern side of central Italy, between the Adriatic Sea and the high Apennine Mountains. Many travelers who come to the Marche are looking for the "authentic" Italy, untarnished by crowds of tourism but welcoming to outsider. The hilltops are strewn with scenic towns and castles, some lending magnificent views all the way to the sea. The Marches are typically known for their seaside beach resorts. The larger resorts tend to have an upbeat feeling with lively nightlife; the main locations are Gabicce Mare, Pesaro, San Benedetto del Tronto, and Senigallia, famous for its 'Velvet Beach'. However, Monte Conero, with its white limestone cliffs and rocky coves, is nothing like any other part of this Adriatic coastline. The primary towns are Urbino, most important for visitors in search of fine Italian art and architecture; Ancona, with its busy seaport and main ferry connection to Croatia, Greece, and Turkey; Pesaro, an appealing seaside resort and a productive town with good shops and beaches; Macerata, famous for its annual outdoor opera festival. Pasta, particularly tagliatelle with a *sugo* (meat sauce), *vincisgrassi*, *a* rich baked lasagna, and *passatelli* strands of pasta made from breadcrumbs, Parmesan cheese, and egg cooked in broth are most prominent. Mountain cured ham and *grigliata mista di carne* (charcoal-grilled meat) are enjoyed most. Along the coast, fresh seafood particularly *brodetto,* a fish stew made with thirteen different varieties of fish, is traditionally served. *Funghi,* nuts, herbs, truffles, and game are widely used in the Marche. The sheep's milk *pecorino di San Leo* cheese is exceptional. When it comes to wine, the Marche is proud of its Verdicchio's, particularly Verdicchio dei Castelli di Jesi and Verdicchio di Matelica. Although this area is known mostly for its white wines, it boasts some excellent reds, mainly Rosso Piceno Superiore, a blend of Montepulciano and Sangiovese grapes.

Umbria: This region is located in the middle of Italy and the only one in central Italy without a coastline. Umbria, often refered to as the "green heart of Italy," is lush and green amid rolling hills and medieval towns such as: Orvieto with its magnificent Gothic *Duomo* (cathedral with dome) and glittering façade; Spoleto, home of the *Festival dei Due Mondi* (Festival of Two Worlds), which is a worldwide attraction that includes music, dance, and theatre scenes; or Assisi, the birth place of St. Francis. Perugia is the region's capital and a very important Etruscan city with stunning architecture such as the Etruscan Arch or the Etruscan Well along with top museums such as Perugia's National Gallery with the best collection of Umbrian art in the world, including a sufficient amount of Perugian paintings. Then there's Gubbio, Todi, Spello, and Città di Castello and several other distinctive hill towns all superbly enhanced by imaginative palaces, monasteries, and churches in addition to producing some of the finest handmade ceramics and savory black truffles. Umbria is home to Lake Trasimeno where you can take a jaunt by boat to one of its islands surrounded by infinite beaches. Umbria's food consists of some basic ingredients: premium olive oil, durham wheat pasta, hog, lamb, and *colombaccio* pigeon. Two specialities of the region are *mazzafegati* sausages made from hog's liver, pine nuts, orange peel, raisins and sugar; *Tartufo Perigord* or black truffle, a mushroom grown beneath the earth and, due to its limited quantity, is one of the most expensive foods in the world. Umbrian's cook a wide range of foods that incorporate fish, meat, vegetables, and cereals including a variety of herbs and spices. This region has long been know for its white wine, particularly Orvieto, but recently the red Torgiano Rosso "riserva" has been appointed a special status while the sweet Vin Santo is highly valued among Umbrians.

Lazio: Roma, the supreme 'Eternal City' is not to be missed. Some principal sights of interest in Rome are Vatican City and its museums that include Raphael's rooms; Sistine Chapel; Basilica of St. Peter and St. Peters square; Villa Borghese; the Colosseum; the Roman Forum; Piazza Navona; Piazza Farnese; the Pantheon; the Jewish Ghetto; Trastevere; and the outdoor market at Campo de' Fiori. Put aside some time for exclusive shopping on the Via Veneto and around the Spanish Steps. According to tradition, throwing a coin into the Trevi Fountain ensures you will return to Rome again. Around Rome there are quite a few interesting places to visit: Tivoli, best known for Villa d'Este with its unique gardens, gravitational water system, and fountains; Frascati and Grottaferrata located in the Castelli Romani hills overlooking the city of Rome which has been a favorite summer retreat of the Romans since the ancient days; Ostia Antica, the old Roman port which has some of the oldest remains in Lazio; Lake Bracciano, the eighth largest lake in Italy with its medieval village of Trevignano, many lakeside cafes, and restaurants; and the Orsini Odescalchi castle dating from the 12th century along with various types of water sports. There are a few Etruscan cities of importance worth visiting such as Cerveteri, Tarquinia, and Viterbo. Visit the Tyrrenian Sea at Civitavecchia especially in summer to relax on the nice sandy beaches and reefs that are a characteristic of its coastline.

The traditional food of Rome and Lazio has always been reliant upon fresh seasonal produce of the nearby countryside: artichokes in spring, mushrooms in autumn, prepared in many different ways, in addition to figs and watermelon that are luscious when in season during the summer months. Many of the authentic Roman dishes are well seasoned with onions, garlic, rosemary, sage, and bay leaves. Pecorino, a flavorful sheep's milk cheese, is often incorporated into dishes while a mild ricotta is used as a filling for pizzas and an ingredient in the Roman dessert *torta di ricotta*. Lazio is the place where the grapevine has been an essential part of life since the Imperial Roman period over 2000 years ago. Frascati is the best known of the local white wines, although Castelli Romani, Marino, Colli Albani, and Velletri are all made from the same grape variety, the Trebbiano. Torre Ercolana is one of the small amount of red wines produced in Lazio and is regarded as one of the region's best wines.

Abruzzo: Abruzzo, together with Molise, form the "ankle" of Italy. This region hugs the Southeastern seaboard with immense sandy beaches extending from the north along the Adriatic directly southward to Pescara. Traveling west from the sea, this region becomes dominated by the Apennines Mountains. This is a land usually thought of as being out-of-the-way and isolated, marked only by desolate hill towns clinging to the sides of mountains. Abruzzo, along with some of the other southern regions, epitomizes a way of life impervious to change for centuries. Here you will find a land of shepherds with uncultivated countryside and desolate castles. Sulmona, an active town with about 25,000 residents, sits 400m above sea level in the center of Abruzzo. It has narrow streets, tree-lined *Piazzas* with imposing houses, especially along Via dell'Ospedale, and displays fine architecture festooned with carved windows and remnants of frescos and sculptures. You will find shops selling blankets, shawls, and sweaters, all made with local wool by the women of Sulmona, whose handiwork is legendary. To the east of Sulmona are the sixty-one peaks and heavily wooded valleys of Maiella National Park offering climbing, skiing, walking, and bird watching. Abruzzo National Park, with its fertile landscape of towering peaks, rivers, lakes, and woodlands is one of the most important in all of Europe, providing refuge for more than forty species of mammals, thirty kinds of reptiles, and three hundred species of birds including the White- Backed Woodpecker and Golden Eagle. Along with opportunities for canoeing, horseback riding, and skiing, a widespread array of trails gives hikers miles of exploration.

The food in Abruzzo is memorable. Their cuisine is highly flavorful mainly with *Peperoncino* (hot red peppers), olive oil, wine, garlic, rosemary, and aromatic saffron which is considered to be the most symbolic of their time-honored cooking. Mushrooms are integrated into almost everything. Shepherding remains the daily way to make a living; therefore, lamb, kid, sheep, and mountain goat are the primary meats served roasted or grilled. Many people still raise their own pigs that produce tasty, lean meat and flavorsome *salami* (cured meat). In seaport areas, fresh fish is incorporated into savory soups that are created from many types of fish. Pasta is most often the first course and *maccheroni alla chitarra* (guitar pasta) is the most typical. Sheets of egg dough are cut with a flat rolling pin on a wooden box with strings. *Pecorino d'Abruzzo*, the local sheep's cheese and a *Burrata,* which is a sphere of luscious mozzarella-like cheese with a soft buttery center, are specialties of this region. Crêpes are traditionally served as dessert, but in Abruzzo, the *scrippelle* are rolled around tasty fillings, placed into broths or served with cheese, vegetables, and meat before baking. The wine vineyards seem to prefer the Montepulciano, Sangiovese, and Trebbiano varieties, producing a wide range of wines including Trebbiano d'Abruzzo, Riesling, Merlot, Chardonnay, and Cabernet.

SOUTHERN ITALY

Molise: This region is located in south-central Italy between the Apennines and the Adriatic coast. Molise is known for its beautiful, natural wilderness and time-honored life style. Its hilly slopes are strewn with castles overlooking medieval villages and ancient ruins. It is divided into two provinces: Campobasso and Isernia. Campobasso, the capitol, is well known for its procession of the "Mysteries," occurring during holy week and marked by somber procession and passion plays. The streets of the town are full of activity with masses of people who come from throughout Italy. The Mysteries are living pictures enacted by men, women, and children, symbolically representing the major feasts of the Church and episodes from the Bible. The town of Isernia rises in the western part of Molise and dates back as far as the prehistoric era when the community of the first Europeans resided in one of its valleys. Isernia is the land which has been unscathed by tourism preserving the anonymity and charm of an unrevealed Italy. Located in Isernia is the Museum of Santa Maria delle Monache, which includes two sections, one dedicated to the Palaeolithic and another to remains from the Samnite period. The town also contains the Sanctuary of St Cosma and St Damian, the Fraterna Fountain, St Peter's Cathedral, and the adjacent entrance hall that comprises a part of the podium of a temple dating back to the days of the Roman Republic. Each year in June, the "donkey race" takes place in the Venafro amphitheater, where contestants ride bareback donkeys and race in a circle. The craft shops of Isernia still create and sell their age-old flutes, bagpipes, and tambourines. The food of Molise is simple, rich in vegetables and pork, seasoned with chili peppers, and tomatoe sauces. Unique to Molise are a white polenta *P'lenta d'iragn* prepared with potatoes, wheat and served with tomato sauce, and *Calconi di ricotta rustica,* which are *ravioli* stuffed with *ricotta* and *provolone* cheeses along with *prosciutto*, then fried in oil. The cheeses of Molise consist primarily of *Mateca*, *Burrino*, and *Scamorza* or *Scamorza Affumicate* (smoked version). Besides the estates of Masseria Di Majo Norante with its DOC Biferno and the table wines of Ramitello, most other wine seems to be enjoyed only locally.

Campania: The historical and renowned beauty of the Campania region is enthralling. Naples, the capital of this province, has numerous sites of cultural and artistic importance. It is home to an aquarium, zoo, Museum of Capodimonte, and the National Archaeological Museum, with one of the worlds most exceptional and interesting collections. Several of Italy's renowned places of exploration are located within this region: Mount Vesuvious, the ancient ruinous civilization of Pompeii and Paestum, the stunning coast of Amalfi, Capri's romantic isle, as well as Sorrento's enchanting peninsula. Furthermore, your day may be spent intermingled with beach hopping, visits to the fashionable towns of Positano and Praiano, or trips to the costal summits of Ravello to admire breath-taking views, along with the magnificent gardens of Villa Cimbrone and Villa Rufolo, the latter gave inspiration for Wagner's Parsifal. Then there's the food, influenced by various civilizations that have come to their shores throughout the centuries, particularly French, Greek, Moorish, and Spanish. Campania is the origin of pizza, tomato sauce, and Spaghetti. Mozzarella cheese and sweet peppers are commonly used ingredients. *Gelateria's* (ice cream shops) are abundant throughout the village streets. Their cuisine is rich and flavorful. Seafood is bountiful and prepared in many distinguished ways, such as *spaghetti con le vongole in salsa bianca* (spaghetti with clams in white sauce) or *cozze in culla*, which are tomatoes that have been cut in half, the pulp scraped out and filled with capers, parsley, oregano, and bread crumbs. The best wines from Campania are the red Turasi sometimes refered to as "the Barolo of the south," the white Fiano di Avellino, the white Greco di Tufo, and the white Falanghina.

Apulia: Also known as Puglia, is the "heel" of the Italian boot, and the Gargano Peninsula is its "spur." Most travelers who venture this far south are most often taking a boat from Brindisi to Greece; however, this is a region full of enjoyable beaches and charming coastal towns. Its relatively flat terrain makes it an ideal region for biking. Bari is the capital and has preserved its ancient maritime traditions through the centuries. Polignano a Mare is a small and fascinating medieval town in the province of Bari on the Adriatic coast. Polignano presents spectacular caves formed as a result of the constant wave motion of the sea that shaped the calcareous rock. Some of the caves are so deep that they extend downwards to the center of the town. The most interesting caves to visit are the Grotta Palazzese, Grotta Stalattitica, and the Grotta della Foca. Some signs of human existence have been found in these caves that date back to the Paleolithic age. Alberobella is a magical land of elf-like conical white washed houses made of stones and held together without mortar called *trulli's*. You can still visit these little unique houses set in the midst of almond and olive trees while watching local residents create ceramics in keeping with the way it was done over five hundred years ago. According to legend, there are two different versions as to why these dry dwellings were constructed. Some declare that the Counts of Puglia insisted they be made in this way enabling them to be easily torn down should the tax inspectors come to collect money from the permanent occupants. Others say because the residents only had to pay for permanent houses, the white stones on top of the roof could be easily removed demonstrating to the inspector that the house was unfinished. Lecce is an impressive city and often referred to as the Florence of the Baroque. Just 20 km north of Gargano is the gem-like small Tremiti Islands, a favorite summer weekend retreat for Italians from the neighboring regions. The islands are accessible only by a one hour boat ride from Termoli, or a three hour ride from Pascara. The entire region is a massive farmland generating cornucopias amounts of tomatoes, grapes, melon, oranges, figs, mandarins, lemons, artichokes, lettuce, wild chicory, fennel, peppers, onions, grains, and olive oil. Puglia is most proud of their pasta, which most often is at the heart of every meal. Italy's best durum wheat is used to produce the region's most celebrated pasta, orecchiette (little ears), along with other cuts that include maccheroni, spaghetti, cavatelli, and small gnocchi. The sea brims with fish, while the pastures are full of cattle and sheep. Sheep's milk cheese is most in abundance especially fresh *ricotta, pecorino*, and their mozzarella-like *burrata di Andria*. Puglia contends with Sicily as the largest wine producer amongst all the regions. Reds and rosés tend to dominate in Puglia, particularly Castel del Monte and the Salento peninsula wines based on the Negroamaro and Malvasia Nera varieties. The long-established whites of Locorotondo and Martina Franca employ the highly valued Verdeca and Bianco d'Alessano varieties.

Basilicata: The Basilicata is surrounded to the north and east by Puglia and the Ionian Sea, to the south with Calabria, and to west with the Tyrrhenian Sea and Campania. Before the Romans conquered Basilicata, this Region was known as Lucania. This is an often overlooked region with mountain scenery that is captivating yet sparse; however, this region has great vacationing possibilities, especially for bona fide travelers. Basilicata contains many places of significant interest: At the lakes of Monticchio walking, biking, boating, and fishing are enjoyable ways to appreciate the beautiful nature and panoramic views; the large sandy shorelines along the Ionian coast contain many picturesque seaside resorts resembling that of the Amalfi coast yet free of tourism; Maratea, with its attractive surrounding villages, is one of the loveliest resorts along this jagged rocky coastline of the south Tyrrhenian Sea and ideal for boating, diving, fishing, swimming, and snorkeling; the Greek ancient ruins of Metaponto and Policoro, archeological digs, hilltop medieval towns, churches, and Renaissance frescoes are as outstanding here as anywhere in Italy. The woodlands and meadows of Basilicata produce bountiful amounts of fruits, vegetables, legumes, cereals, and herbs with splendid fragrances, especially cumin, chives, rosemary, mints, and wild fennel. The sheep and goat feed on these aromatic herbs producing very savory meats, which are then grilled, braised, or baked. The sausages throughout many of the regions are often called *luganega*, in honor of Lucania's celebrated and flavorsome specialty. To delight in the tastes of the region try a variety of their spicy sausage. Cheeses are a regular part of their daily meals. The Lucanian pecorino cheese is a blend of 70 percent sheep's milk and 30 percent goat's milk, which is aged from three months to one year. It is an extremely delectable cheese. Many other remarkable cheeses are still produced by time-honored methods, some of which are: *ricotta, burrata, mozzarella, scamorza, manteca,* buffalo-milk cheese, and *caciocavallo*. Historical sources have recognized this region as one of the first places where the grapevine emerged in Italy. The Greeks brought the Aglianico vine to Basilicata possibly as long ago as the sixth or seventh centuries. Grown on the slopes of the extinct volcano Monte Vulture, this full-bodied, deep colored wine has become even more sophisticated and complex in flavor through time. There are also some new and original variations of the wine, which include a semi-sweet as well as sparkling wine; however, the dry Vecchio or Riserva, aged in oak barrels, are most esteemed. In Matera and other parts of the Basilicata, reds from Sangiovese, Montepulciano and Aglianico are used for table wine. Two praise-worthy white wines are the sweet Moscato and Malvasia, particularly from the Vulture zone and the eastern Bradano valley.

Calabria: Calabria encompasses the tip of Italy's peninsula, bordered by Basilicata to the north and extending down between the Tyrrhenian and the Ionian Seas towards Sicily, from which the Strait of Messina divides it. The inland area is scattered with small picturesque villages embracing the hills that slope down to meet the water, along with attractive citrus plantations and olive groves. Calabria has extraordinary landscapes across rugged mountains, infinite wheat fields, and dazzling clear seas. Here is a region with one of the most unrestricted coastline beaches in Europe ideal for boating, swimming, and fishing. Traveling inland towards La Sila Grande you will come across miles of evergreen forests with snow-capped mountains, streams, and waterfalls. Calabria is home to two national parks: Aspromonte National Park, made up of crystalline granite resembling an enormous pyramid, and Pollino National Park, home to many rare plants and animal species while being the largest protected area amongst the recent parks established in Italy. Calabria is one of the regions that has stayed most true to its heritage. In the small villages, elderly men still spend much time playing cards at tables in the towns piazzas, as the older woman still dressed in black sit together near their homes to chat about the local news. The food of Calabria, even with an abundance of fresh fish, consists of fresh pastas, vegetables cooked in a variety of ways, and meats, mainly pork. Calabria holds pasta in the highest regard, with each city or town specializing in its own pasta. Calabrians pride themselves in knowing the best sauce to combine with each pasta in creating the tastiest dishes. Sauces include a wide array of seafood and meats in addition to a variety of vegetables, most importantly tomatoes. Black pepper and peperoncini are extensively used as seasonings that give Calabrian food their notorious spicy flavor. *Spaghetti alle Vongole*, Spaghetti with clams, is the ideal summer dish commonly served in Calabria. This region's wines are known for their excellence as well as their high alcohol content. Among the best-known wine is Cirò, which grows low down in the hills along the Ionian coast between the ancient Greek cities of Sibari and Crotone. A legend is told that Krimisa, the wine drank by the Calabrian athletes in celebration of their victories in the early Olympiads, is the precursor to Cirò. Two important grape varieties of Greek origin are the red Gaglioppo wine and white Greco wine.

Sicily: Sicily is the largest island in the Mediterranean and is considered the most important economically along with its rich heritage of history and art. The island is encircled by the Tyrrhenian Sea to the north; the Ionian Sea to the east, the Sicilian Sea to the southwest, and the Strait of Messina separates it from Calabria. Sicily is the most expansive region in Italy. It combines with the outlying Pelagie Island, Ustica, Egadi, Pantelleria, and the Aeolian Islands which consist of seven major islands: Lipari, Salina, Stromboli, Panarea, Vulcano, Alicudi, and Filicudi. On the Aeolian Islands you'll find stunning panoramas, volcanoes, ancient castles, archeological museums, a variety of water sports, excellent fishing, and fine beaches. Sicily abounds with many wonderful places of interest to see: Agrigento is a city of exceptional archeological heritage; Catania is positioned on the Gulf of Catania and stretches over the southern base slopes of Europe's highest active volcano, Mt. Etna; Ragusa is one of the most authentic Sicilian areas, with quintessential towns, magnificent wide sandy beaches, and crystal clear seas; Syracuse exudes a strong connection with its ancient Greek past, mythologically as well as historically; Palermo is Sicily's largest and most sophisticated city while Taormina is a captivating medieval town with unrivaled views of Mount Etna and the Ionian coast along with a true chic ambiance. The cuisine of Sicily is distinctively unusual from most other Italian regions. The Greeks, Romans, Arabs, Normans, French, and Spanish have all had some bearing on the foods of Sicily. Its imaginative combination of sweet and sour essences, bounteous use of aromatic herbs, fresh abundant seafood, and decadent desserts, along with its succulent citrus fruits, set apart Sicilian cooking from all others. The basic ingredients used most frequently are olive oil, pasta, fresh fruits, and vegetables. Some typical Sicilian antipasti are: *Caponata*, which is a pâté like mixture of eggplant and other Mediterranean ingredients that is enjoyed served on crusty bread, and *Arancini*, which are fried rice balls stuffed with beef, chicken, and cheese. Some other characteristic dishes that incorporate the typical produce of the land are: *Spaghetti alla Norma,* prepared with fried eggplants, basil, and *ricotta salata* cheese; *Tonno con Capperi* tuna with capers; *Sfinciune*, a focaccia served with chopped onions, tomatoes, anchovies, and cheese; and *Pesci Spada con Salsa Arancione*, swordfish with orange sauce. Sicilian desserts are outstanding: *Cannolis* are cylinder like pastries stuffed with sweet and creamy ricotta cheese; *Cassata* is the most adored Sicilian cake, usually served at Easter and is filled with the identical rich *ricotta* filling; *cubbaita*, a nougat with honey, almonds, and sesame seeds; and of course, Sicilian *gelato* (ice cream) is exceptional. Sicily is considered one of the earliest winemaking cultures in the world. Today it continues to play a major role in Italian winemaking with a wide variety of sweet wines, mainly Marsala, Malvasia delle Lipari, and Moscato, along with some reds and whites that include Spumantes, Cabernet Sauvignon, Merlot, Chardonnay, Sangiovese, and Rosato.

Sardinia: Sardinia is the second largest island and is situated in the middle of the Western Mediterranean just 12 km from Corsica. Modern-day Sardinia is the beloved holiday site of the exceedingly affluent Italians. If your first choice is to spend a holiday surrounded by countless beautiful sandy beaches and small islands with turquoise seas while being witness to some of the most spectacular scenery, Sardinia's Costa Smeralda is the place for you. There are a host of other attractions to enjoy while on the island, such as sailing, reef diving, water-skiing, scuba diving, wind surfing, fishing, biking, mountain climbing, visiting archeological ruins, and boutique shopping. The resort towns of Porto Rotundo and Porto Cervo are filled with designer shops, cafes and restaurants. Alghero is considered one of the loveliest towns in Sardegna and has preserved the architecture as well as the language of its Catalonian past. La Maddalena Archipelago has some beaches and innumerable historical sites, of which Garibaldi's final home and resting place on the island of Caprera is nearby. Then there's the natural sandstone formations of Santa Teresa di Gallura, the town of Castelsardo with its ancient towers and fortifications, the Doria Castle, and the 12th century church of Santa Maria di Tergu. Surprisingly, Sardinians are people of the land where their main focal point has been that of shepherds and farmers. Sardinian cuisine is a blend of both land and sea centered on bread, pasta, wine, cheese, olive oil, and sweets. Roasting meat, particularly sheep, lamb, and pig along with fish, is a common preparation which retains the tenderness of the meat while cooking it to perfection. Other specialties include artichokes, wild mushrooms, saffron and, of course, their prized *Pecorino* cheese produced from sheep or goat, animals that today still roam the same uncontaminated terrain that they have for centuries generating the identical mild and delicious flavors of ancient Sardinia. Alghero is famous for lobster typically prepared by boiling and simply served with olive oil, salt, and a hint of lemon or incorporated into a sauce over pasta. Every special feast-day such as Carnival, Christmas and Easter has its own unique desserts. The basic ingredients of Sardinia's deserts are typically almonds, oranges, lime peels, cinnamon, vanilla, raisins, walnuts, sugar, and honey. Often *ricotta* or freshly grated *pecorino* is incorporated. Up until the last three decades, growing grapes and wine manufacturing techniques were carried on as they had since the vine first appeared in Sardina, unaffected by the modern world. The grapes are first harvested, then transported back by mule, and finally squeezed by walking on them with bare feet. Some of Sardinia's most renowned wines are the reds and roses consisting of Cannonau, Monica, and Carignano, while white wines comprise Vermentino, Semidano, and Nuragus. The dessert wines include Malvasia, Nasco, and Vernaccia.

For additional details and information on everything Italy, contact:
ENIT "Italian State Tourist Board" at www.enit.it
Or telephone directly:
Canada +416-925-4882
Italy +39-649711
United Kingdom +44-20-73551557
United States +212-245-5618

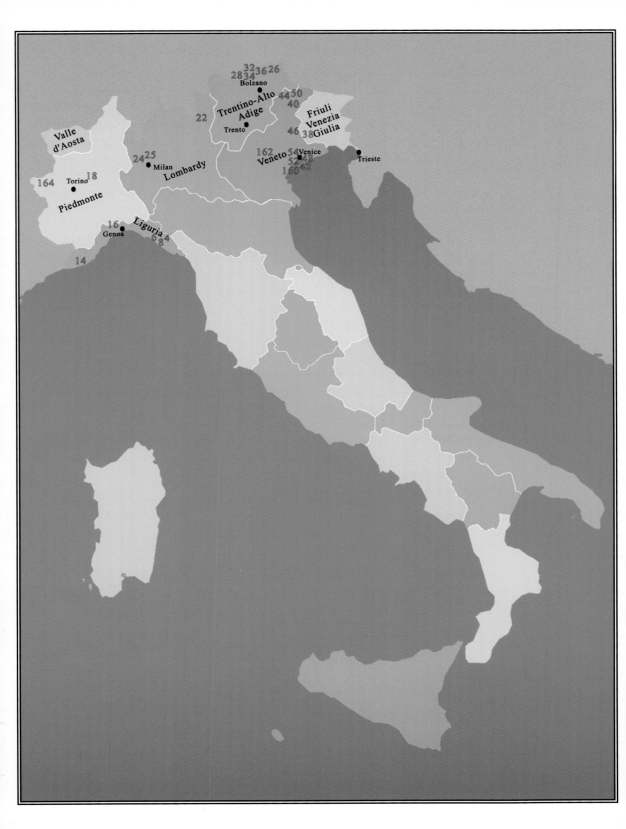

Valle
d'Aosta

Torino 18
164
Piedmonte

Genoa
16
Liguria 4
6 8
14

24 25
Milan
Lombardy

28 32 36 26
34
Bolzano
Trentino-Alto
22 Adige
Trento

44 50
40
Friuli
Venezia
46 38 Giulia

162 54 Venice
52 48
Veneto
160 42
Trieste

Northern Italy

A portion of the 1,207 kilometer Dolomite Mountain Super Ski area

The resort town of Cortina d`Ampezzo

Ca` Peo

Owner: Melly, Francesco and Nicoletta Solari
Via dei Caduti, 80 / 16040 Chiavari a Leivi (Ge) / Italy
Telephone: ++390185319696 / Fax: ++390185319671
E-Mail: nicosol@libero.it / Web: www.capeo.it

★★★ **Price guide:** €104 • Major credit cards accepted **Amenities:** Air conditioning • Bar • Cable/Satellite TV • Internet • Airport: Genova • Nearby towns: Santa Margherita Ligure • Rapallo • Portofino • Chiavari • Restaurant Association: Union e Ristoranti Del Buon Ricordo: Breakfast included, lunch & dinner à la carte, closed Mondays & Tuesdays for lunch • Total rooms: 5; 3 suites & 2 apartments **Activities:** Biking • Golf: Rapallo 15km • Hiking • Shopping • Swimming & Tennis: 7 km **Additional Information:** Unione Ristoranti del (Buon Ricordo) Closed all of November • Special food preparation for kids • Additional bed: €25 • Crib: free

The Etruscan antique fair is presently held in Lucca. We spent the afternoon exploring the immensely charming city while searching for valuable heirlooms. Isaac negotiated well for a miniature antique *gondola* (venitian boat) which required him to use the Italian he had learned over the past month. Our final purchase was freshly made black licorice from a street kiosk. Be forewarned, although the licorice tastes wonderful, it may have a laxative effect, which was precisely what happened.

We departed Lucca mid-afternoon for our next one night accommodation at Ca`Peo, in the small mountain village of Chiavari a Leivi, south of Genova. Knowing of their reputation as celebrated members of the exclusive restaurant organization, *Unione Ristoranti del Buon Ricordo,* I was raring to experience their legendary cuisine. However, with our need for numerous bathroom stops, by the time we arrived their kitchen had closed for the evening. Regardless of this fact, the owners, Melly, Francesco, and Nicoletta Solari, united to create a warm Italian family welcome with dinner. Francesco's kind reception and willingness to serve us further enhanced his wife's culinary genius. As a true lover of the "art of food," my imagination was stimulated, leaving my pallet yearning for more. The diminutive size of Cá Peo's farmhouse makes for an intimate experience. Their dining room consists of nine tables with vistas of the sea and mountains. An additional building of more modern construction contains five small suites.

We awoke the following morning to a sweeping panoramic view of the surrounding Gulf of Tigullio. The Solari family continued their fine intimate hospitality with breakfast set forth on the terrace. Cá Peo is approximately a half hour drive to the seaside resorts of Rapallo and Santa Margherita, making it a good alternative to the busier spots.

Hotel Continental

Owner: Family Ciana

Via Pagana, 8 / 16038 Santa Margherita Liguria (Genova) / Italy

Telephone: ++390185286512 / Fax: ++390185284463

E-Mail: continental@hotel-continental.it / Web: www.hotel-continental.it

★★★★ **Price guide:** €67-€150 per person **Amenities:** Air conditioning • Bar • Cable/Satellite TV • Internet • Laundry • Airport: Genova • Nearby towns: Santa Margherita Ligure, Rapallo and Portofino • Restaurant: Breakfast included; lunch & dinner à la carte • Total rooms: 76 **Activities:** Boat rentals • Golf: Rapallo 4km • Horseback riding: 4km Rapallo • Private beach • Shopping • Tennis court: 4km Rapallo **Additional Information:** On bus stop • Pets allowed: €15 • Meeting rooms • Parking outside: €11; garage: €16 • Half board/full board

This is an exceptional location to enjoy and appreciate the Italian Rivera and the exceptional Cinque Terre nestled between palms and pines with an outstanding position over the sea. Although situated in the lovely town of Santa Margherita, Portofino is in eye's view. Gardens abound as you descend towards their private beach inclusive of a snack bar. Hotel Continental is a modern, high quality seventy-six room resort. The best rooms are those located directly on the terraces offering a Ligurian Sea view. Every room is complete with air conditioning, TV, telephone, and mini-bar.

The restaurant has a bird's eye view of the Ligurian coast and terraced hills. Their food and service is of high standards. Many sports activities can be arranged through the concierge, such as golfing in nearby Rapallo, or tennis and horseback riding. The sea avails itself to swimming, sailing, snorkeling, or scuba diving.

Hotel Continental sits just on the outskirts of the town. A quick three-minute walk places you in Santa Margherita's main piazza, a delightful place to relax and eat gelato while the kids enjoy the park's swings and scooter about.

We loved being on the Cape of Santa Margherita. It is less known than its neighboring town of Portofino, with sensational *pasticceria* (pastry shops), restaurants, and artful shops. Boats inhabit the cove in front of the main square. The beach itself brims with stones, as does most of the coast. The boys collected numerous pieces that they brought home to assemble into water fountains, a nice memento of their journey.

Hotel Porto Roca

Manager/Owner: Guerrina Arpe
Via Corone, 1 / Monterosso al Mare / Cinque Terre / 19016 (SP) / Italy
Telephone: ++390187817502 / Fax: ++390187817692
E-Mail: portoroca@cinqueterre.it / Web: www.portoroca.it

★★★★ **Price guide:** €260–€430 • Major credit cards accepted **Amenities:** Air conditioning • Baby sitting by arrangement • Bar • Cable/Satellite TV • Internet • Laundry • Airport: Genova • Nearby towns: Santa Margherita Ligure, La Spezia, Portofino, and the Cinque Terre. • Restaurant: Breakfast included; lunch & dinner à la carte • Total rooms: 43 **Activities:** Boat rentals • Fishing • Hiking: Cinque Terre • Massage: by request • Private sea beach • Shopping **Additional Information:** Directly on the hiking trail of the Cinque Terre • Half board/full board

Time and again I am asked, "What is your favorite place in Italy?" This inquiry is comparable to, "Who is your most beloved child?" I love all of Italy. Every locality brims with its own virtues. The Cinque Terre, however, has a position in our hearts that at times possesses a matchless comparison to anywhere we have ever been. Inevitably, the boys will ask, "Are we going to the Cinque this trip?"

Our favorite place to stay is Hotel Porto Roca, a paradise set above the sea at the mouth of the renowned footpath that connects the Cinque Terre villages of Monterosso, Vernazza, Corniglia, Manarola, and Riomaggiore. Monterosso, the western most of the villages, is perhaps the best prepared for tourists in the Cinque Terre: warm and friendly hospitality, vast shops and restaurants providing dishes distinctive of the ligurian coast.

Sitting amidst their garden terrace or on your personal balcony overlooking the beach and port of Monterosso gives you the sense of sailing upon the water. The antique furnishings bestow the feeling of staying in an old yet elegant villa. It's forty-three modern air-conditioned rooms offer TV, telephone, safety deposit box, and mini-bar. The staff is warm and efficient.

On the beach below the hotel, lounge chairs and sun umbrellas are set-aside exclusively for the guests of Porto Roca. Enjoying evening swims in the sea after an invigorating hike through the Cinque is a great finishing point to your day.

Dining in their expansive panoramic restaurant is a treat. The service and fresh cuisine featuring traditional and typical local dishes are impeccable. Fish caught in the water directly beneath the hotel accompanied by outstanding Cinque Terre wines are reminiscent of our stay.

❧ The Cinque Terre ❧

DAVID'S VIEW

One area that keeps drawing us back is the Cinque Terre. When I think of the Cinque, I envision some of the most breathtaking views of the sea from high jagged cliffs. The colors of the Mediterranean vary from dark blues to emerald green, bordered by white from the sea crashing into the rocks that line the beach. If you did nothing else but sit and watch the sunrise and sunset and the movement of the surf, it would have been a memorable experience. But if you venture to walk the five towns, you will see and taste things as they may have been a hundred years ago.

The five towns are built into the cliffs as they reach down to the sea. They are pastel colored and beckon to be photographed or painted. The five towns are connected only by railroad and foot trail. This alone is what makes the Cinque Terre special for it remains unspoiled by progress and modernization. The northern town of Monterosso and the southern town of Riomaggiore are separated by only twelve kilometers. You can travel them by train in about thirty minutes or walk from town to town in about one half a day because they are all about two to five kilometers apart from each other. The walk is invigorating because the trails go up and down the cliffs. You'll walk through tunnels, terrace vineyards, lemon groves, and the gardens and yards of the towns people's homes. You'll see the locals walking with their groceries and selling their homegrown fruits. At times, you'll be 200 meters above the sea or on a trail just a stone's throw from the beach. Sometimes the trail will only be wide enough for one person to walk; other times you will use carefully placed stones making a staircase to climb up and down the cliffs. It will challenge the avid hiker yet Ari, at age six, was able to enjoy the entire walk. The first time Debra and I walked the Cinque, we were by ourselves. We missed the kids and wished they were with us because we knew they would love all that it offered.

The complete walk from Riomaggiore, the eastern-most village, to Monterosso, the western-most village, takes approximately five to seven hours. The least challenging part of the route starts from the railway station square and proceeds along the *Via Del Amore*, or the lover's pathway, to Manarola, a thirty minute walk. In Manarola, it gently rises then levels off along a beautiful bridle path bringing you to the Corniglia railway station. Corniglia, at this point, continues on to the center of the village where you will climb steps, approximately one hour outside of Corniglia. The footpath remains at somewhat the same level. There are some challenging points along the way and then it descends into Vernazza, taking one hour and thirty minutes. The last leg of the journey is the longest and most difficult. This two-hour route reaches a height of 180 meters and then sharply drops down to Monterosso.

The most obvious change that I see when we revisit here is the increase in the number of tourists. It is not uncommon to walk the trails and hear people speaking English. We've even encountered fellow Atlantans on the trail. Modern life is making its way there, with Internet cafés popping up in nearby towns such as Monterosso and Vernazzza.

It's a good idea to make reservations before arriving because hotel rooms are limited. Another option for the daring is to rent a room or apartment from a local resident. This can be arranged at the Information Center in Monterosso. These accommodations are generally very clean but also very basic. We prefer the Hotel Porto Roca (Northern Italy). It has a great location high above the sea, and just a five-minute walk from the town of Monterosso. The first time we visited here with the kids, we didn't have a reservation. The hotel was booked, but there was one room for guests who had not yet arrived. The hotel informed us they would release it at 6:00 p.m. We asked them how many people it accommodated to which they replied that it had one queen bed and two bunk beds. Since we were two adults and three kids, we figured we could squeeze in the room.

Precisely at 6:00 p.m., just when the manager was inviting us to take the room, we heard a child screaming and crying. Ari ran into the hotel yelling that some hornets had stung Isaac. A moment later, Isaac arrived. His hand was swollen, and he cried as he described that he was playing on the cliff and had reached for a rock that was hiding a hornet's nest. Well, the staff was very kind, and they attended to him quickly and promptly, making him feel more comfortable. When everything calmed down, the manager said that he wasn't aware that we had two kids, but imagine his surprised to learn we actually have three. There was a quiet moment of embarrassment, and then the manager smiled and told us that we all could be accommodated. We went on to have an incredible meal, a very restful sleep, and a wonderful beach day.

For entertainment that night, we walked down the cliff from the hotel and watched the locals play *bocce* at their private bocce ball club. They were very skilled players, and they entertained us with their typical animated gestures with their hands and loud bickering over the many questionable calls. Every decision became a theatrical production as to who scored the last point. The games appear endless carrying on into the early morning hours, and perhaps all the way through to the next generation.

We play a game with the kids when we walk between the five towns of the Cinque Terre. We usually take about an hour to get from one town to the next so, upon arrival, we reward the children with Italian fare. Sometimes we have a gelato, or pizza, or cappuccino. I like to take a swim or check out an Internet café to check our e-mail. One of my most memorable lunches was sitting on the rocks in Vernazzi, watching the kids swim. We shared a $3.00 bottle of wine, some *Gorgonzola dolce* (sweet blue cheese), a fresh tomato, and some olives accompanied by fresh bread. The cost for the entertainment, exercise, best table in the house, and gourmet cuisine for two adults and three kids amounted to about $12.00. Memory and experience... priceless!

For the adventurous type, there is a somewhat eccentric man who owns a private beach and campground on the outskirts of Corniglia. When we were by ourselves, Debra and I ventured to it. A sign in front of an abandoned railroad tunnel leads through the mountain to the beach. It's written in Italian, but we interpreted it to say that there was a 5.00 *lire* charge to ride through the tunnel to the beach. I didn't think it was worth the money so I convinced Debra and two American students who were touring Europe for the summer to walk with me. After about fifty yards, it became pitch black and we couldn't even see our feet. It was so eerie that we immediately turned around and went back to the entrance. At that moment, the owner drove up in his pickup truck and explained to us that it cost 5.00 *lire* to go to his beach. Our curiosity was aroused, so we paid him, hopped into his truck, and drove through the tunnel with his headlights on. It was about a half-mile trip, which we realized we never would have made without a flashlight.

When we arrived to the other side, we found a small but nice beach. There were a few nude bathers and sunbathers. This was a very secluded and private cove. The owner had about ten acres of land that he was developing into some primitive campsites. They were actually quite picturesque, and they were all at different terrace levels overlooking the sea. The distance between the beach and the trail we were on was about three hundred feet. It looked like there was a path that we could take back up to the road, so once again I talked Debra into hiking up the trail with me to avoid having to pay the 5.00 *lire* to get back out through the tunnel; it was a matter of principle rather than finances Well, after about an hour of hiking and climbing, we realized that with only fifty feet to go, we were never going to make it to the top of the road because the vegetation was like jungle, and the cliff became extremely steep. We were so close yet so far. Tired and dejected, we walked back to the entrance to the tunnel. The owner was sitting there under an umbrella drinking a Heineken. His expression said it all. He knew once we came into his beach, you had to pay to get off his beach. So I walked up to him with my 5.00 *lire*, he took it and smiled. I said, "We're ready to go. Should we get into the truck?" He didn't say anything but walked over to the tunnel, opened up a metal box on the wall, and flicked on a switch, which, to our amazement, lit up the whole tunnel. We had a nice walk back out through the tunnel, back to the trail.

Through the years we have gathered a collection of Cinque Terre stones from the sea, which is displayed in a rustic Tuscan wooden bowl on the mantle in our bedroom. Now and then I see Debra pick up one of these mementos, handle it as she would a costly precious gem, perhaps appreciating it more for its sentimental meaning than its intrinsic value.

Hotel Punta Est

Owner: Podestá Family / Manager: Attilio Podestá
Via Aurelia 1 / I-17024 Finale Ligure / Sovana, Italy
Telephone/Fax: ++39019600611-2-3
E-Mail: info@puntaest.com / Web: www.puntaest.com

★★★★ **Price guide:** €150–€420 • Major credit cards accepted **Amenities:** Air conditioning • Bar • Internet • Airports: Genova; Nice, France • Nearby town: Finale Ligure, Garlenda • Restaurant: Breakfast included; lunch & dinner à la carte • Total rooms: 40 plus suites **Activities:** Biking • Boat rentals • Fishing • Golf at Garlenda Country Club • Hiking • Climbing • Horseback riding • Massage: Sha-Tsu, Ayurveda & reflexology • Private sea beach • Swimming pool **Additional Information:** Open: April-mid-October • Meeting facilities • Belly dancing • Chi Kung Shaolin • Piano bar: Maestro Giovanni • Half board/full board

Punta Est is an 18th century Genovese villa enveloped by an expansive park overlooking the Ligurian Sea and expanding upward to the Maritime Alps. This four-star hotel puts forward all the comforts and amenities guaranteeing a triumphant family holiday!

Attilio Podesta, the owner, perpetuates the existence of this magnificent hotel located 100 kilometers from the French border on the Ligurian "Riviera Della Palme." He appears to be everywhere simultaneously; nevertheless, he's present and attentive to all his guests' needs. His personality and honest nature is as attractive as his domain.

The hotel contains forty rooms ranging from the more private and romantic in the original villa to the extra spacious ones in the newer building. Whichever accommodation you choose will afford you a view of the park and sea. Whether positioned on a terrace, swimming in the pool or dining at the restaurant, an idyllic vista awaits you. It is no wonder why Professor Delachi, a composer and musician at La Scala in Milan, found solace in this, his summer home, in the 1930s.

Winding down the pathways from the hotel, you would discover a huge natural cave filled with stalactites and stalagmite crystal. The Podesta families have brilliantly transformed this grotto into a remarkable meeting spot. Here in this modern yet prehistoric dwelling, the family can relax, have a drink, and appreciate music or special performances offered by Punta Est. Across from the cave is a tunnel below the highway, giv-

ing your family safe access to the public beach and private area with lounge chairs. Should you need a diversion from this peaceful scene, bicycling, hiking, scaling the cliffs of Cape Noli and Perti, horseback riding, sightseeing, the marina, and golf are at hand. David appreciated the opportunity to play the picturesque and well-maintained golf course at Garlenda. We joined him at the completion of his round for an unforgettable family style meal at Ristorante IL Frantoio where the *specialitá* is Paella Valenciana. It is located on Via Lerrone 56. The phone number is ++390182582046. However, for our family, all we required was the chance to swim in the Mediterranean Sea, run on the beach, dive off the rocks, and snorkel while searching for undiscovered sea life. Link all the activity with Punta Est's famed gastronomic dishes presented with choice local and natural wines, and you have an unrivaled Mediterranean quality vacation.

Palazzo Fieschi

Proprietor/Director: Aldo & Simonetta Caprile and daughter, Sarah
Piazza della Chiesa, 14 / 16010 Savignone (Genova) / Italy
Telephone: ++390109360063 / Fax: ++39010936821
E-Mail: fieschi@split.it / Web: www.palazzofieschi.it

★★★ **Price guide:** €90-€150 per person • Residenza d' Epoca **Amenities:** Bar • Cable/Satellite TV • Internet • Restaurant: Breakfast included; dinner à la carte • Total rooms: 21 **Activities:** Biking • Children's park • Fishing: nearby • Golf: 25 km • Horseback riding • Shopping • Cultural tours **Additional Information:** Tours of Cinque Terre, Cantine del Gavi, and Genova • Shopping outlets: Serranalle Scrivia

Palazzo Fieschi is located in Savignone, a realistic Italian village northeast of Genoa. This 15th century palace was the residence of Savignone Lords and the noble Fieschi family. Carlotta Fieschi was the last descendent of the family to reside here. Since 1856, this *Residenza d'Epoca* stands as the most ancient working hotel in Liguria. To paraphrase Goffredo Casalis of Palazzo Fieschi, "Its location at the east side of the square of Savignone is the ideal background of the oldest performance in the world, man's life, played in a masterly fashion by a unique main character... history."

Palazzo Fieschi has twenty pleasant rooms, many of which offer alpine views with goats on the hillside. All are equipped with bathtub or shower, TV, and telephone; however, the most unforgettable feature of this Palazzo is

Simonetta's outstanding culinary flare. Ristorante Palazzo Fieschi is a member of *Del Conservatorio Delle Cucine Mediterranee*, which is a Genoa based organization that invites chefs who maintain only the highest level of standards according to their set regulations. Foremost is the exclusive use of fresh local biological, natural ingredients. We could not have chosen a more superb setting to celebrate my forty-fifth birthday! Simonetta says, "Cooking time is longer than usual but not too much in order to benefit taste and all your senses!" The utilization of local traditional products such as *olio extra vergine D' oliva* (olive oil), *tomini* and *ricotta* (both soft cheeses) of Savignone, sausages of the valley, mushrooms, chestnuts, and their revered *Quarantina* (potatoes) are used only during the current season. Her *I nostri gnocchi di quarantine al castelmagno* (potato dumplings with regional cheese) remains unrivaled.

The village of Savignone has many authentic sights to see. Saunter through the Piazza della Chiesa and visit the dressmaker, butcher, and baker. The Museo delgi Alpini is a modest museum containing photographs, documents, uniforms, helmets, and other information that serves as an historical account of Savignone's past events and people. In the evening be a spectator to a bona fide game of *bocce* ball while sitting courtside at the local café enjoying *gelato*, *espresso*, or an after-dinner *digestivo*. On Sunday mornings, local vendors and families frequently assemble to buy, sell, and trade their goods. During our stay, the annual Fiat 500 rally was taking place. The village became lively as droves of these automobile *affezionati* (lovers) rolled into Palazzo Fieschi's

garden with true Italian panache to display and compete for the best in its class.

In contrast to some of the chic towns of the Italian Riviera, this is not the place you go to "see and be seen." Instead, this Hamlet provides your family with an historic perspective of life unchanged by modernization. The advantage to staying here, at Palazzo Fieschi, is its close proximity to the sea and bustling metropolis of Genoa, balanced by the tranquil atmosphere of a mountain haven.

Locanda Del Sant`Uffizio

Owner: Turin Hotels International / Director: Vito Andrisini
Strada Sant'Uffizio, 1 / 14030 Cioccaro di Penango-Asti / Italy
Telephone: ++390141916292 / Fax: ++390141916068
E-Mail: santuffizio@thi.it / Web: www.thi.it

★★★★ **Price Guide:** €161-€285 • Major credit cards accepted **Amenities:** Air conditioning • Bar • Cable/Satellite TV • Internet • Airport: Genova • Nearby towns: Calliano, Casale, Moncalvo, Monferrato, and Turin • Restaurant: Breakfast included. Lunch & dinner à la carte. • Total rooms: 33 plus suites **Activities:** Golf at Margara Golf Club • Gym • Swimming pool • Tennis court • Cultural tours **Additional Information:** Luxury break packages • Open all year

This 17th century ancient monastery just southeast of Turin is an ideal stay for a magical family holiday as well as the 2006 Winter Olympic games! The scenic hillside route towards Locanda del Sant'Uffizio is cloaked in vineyards and is often referred to as the wine route. While the area is the Piedmont region, the hotel is located in the center of the Monferrato district. These gently rolling limestone hills produce the famous Asti wines, Gorgonzola cheese, and excellent *bianco tartufi* (white truffles). Your kids will marvel as you journey through hilltop villages individually protected by its own castles. You will enjoy discovering an area rich in history, culture, and imaginative cuisine.

The Locanda and pool sit amidst ornate Italian

gardens. Uffizio's cultivated ornamental grounds, accompanied by aromatic scents of roses, lemons, and oranges, bring about a spiritual calmness. Whether we were swimming, biking, exercising, or playing tennis, this tranquility prevailed throughout. Uffizio's ecclesiastical roots are evident purely in its ancient architectural remains.

Sant'Uffizio's thirty-three rooms are a luxurious blend of antique furnishings with every modern comfort and convenience. Vito Andresini manages this Locando with love and care. His fondness and respect for children are apparent through his relationship with his young son. Each Sunday, his wife and child come to spend the day while he works, regularly taking a moment to kiss and hug his family, but never missing an operational detail.

The territory of Asti is one of the smallest in Italy; however, it has the largest aggregation of first class restaurants. Il Ristorante della Locanda del Sant'Uffizio is the best known, holding a one Michelin-star rating. Cooking in this region is done primarily with butter. A favored dish is fonduta featuring their beloved tartufi Bianchi (white truffle) cheese, milk, and eggs. Last spring in Georgia, my boys planted a vegetable garden.

Most importantly, they grew *courgette* (zucchini) for the single purpose of harvesting the bright yellow tulip-like *fiori* (flowers) that are revered throughout nearly all of Italy, but generally discarded by most in the United States. The Romans stuff them with fresh mozzarella cheese, and anchovies then batter dip the flowers for frying to a perfect crispness. The Venetians tend to prepare the flower in *risotto* (rice) with garlic, onion, dry white wine, and Parmigiano-Reggiano cheese. If you have yet to taste this culinary delight, Sant'Uffizio's inspired recipes will tantalize your pallets. Breakfast at this Locanda was outstanding with a splendid wide assortment of local fresh produce that included savory cheeses, unequaled to anything we've experienced.

This Turin area has many excursions and sights worth seeing. For automotive aficionados, there is the motor museum with its collection of cars, chassis, engines and historical documentation. Tour the castle of Monferrato, visit Romanesque churches and the famous Abbey of Vezzolano. At Locanta del Sant'Uffizio, you will feel welcomed by their genuine hospitality based upon their authentic regional Piedmonte tradition.

❧ *Debra on Food & Kids* ❧

The distinguishing feature of Italian cooking is the use of fresh ingredients that are simply cooked maintaining their original essence and freshness. The use of a variety of flavors and rich inventiveness in preparation will appeal to the untrained palate as well as the most demanding gourmet. The beauty of traveling in Italy with kids is that pasta, pizza, and *patate fritte* (French fries) are always readily available.

A typical day will begin with *Colazione* (Italian breakfast) which compared to an American or English breakfast is typically light: *cappuccino* (coffee and steamed milk) and a *brioche* (sweet pastry), or just *espresso* (black short strong coffee). *Pranzo* (lunch) is traditionally the largest meal beginning with an *antipasto* (appetizer) followed by a *primo piatto* (first course) pasta, rice, or soup, a *secondo piatto* (second course) of meat or fish with *verdura o insalate* (vegetable or salad), then *frutta* (fresh fruit) and *dolci* (desserts), ending with *espresso* and possibly a *grappa* or *amaro* (digestive liqueur) *Cena* (dinner) is similar to lunch. Currently there is a trend towards having a light lunch and then dinner turns into the major meal.

If your children are unaccustomed to a European diet and eat only limited types of foods, take on the plane unopened boxes of their favorite cereals, crackers, and snack foods until you can find a *COOP*, which is an Italian supermarket where you can stock up on a variety of supplies. They tend to be on the outskirts of larger towns. The food needs to remain sealed until you go through customs in Italy. Carry these provisions with you to ensure your kids always have their familiar foods available: bring their favorite cereal to breakfast, or peanut butter, jelly, and crackers to lunch. A word to the wise… expecting your kids to be suddenly open to and interested in different varieties of food if they have never been expose to diverse cuisine is unrealistic. We have traveled with many families who honestly had this type of anticipation for their kids and it tends to create tension, frustration, and disappointment for all. On the other hand, we have also experienced the complete reverse scenario: When we were at Locanda Del Sant'Uffizio (Northern Italy), a couple, Tricia and Adam, were touring with their six-month-old son, Garrett. He will have been in ten different countries by the time he is one year. As they sat in the formal dining room enjoying duck l' orange, pasta with truffles, and zucchini flowers, Garrett was reaching for the food off their plate, establishing and acquiring a taste early on for a variety of different foods.

🐦 *David on Food* 🐦

I remember the first time I saw a fruit stand in Italy. The lemons were the size of grapefruits. The fruits and vegetables there aren't just enormous; they are also the best tasting fruit in the world. For me each season when a new fruit ripens is cause for celebration.

I live in Georgia, the peach state, but the best peach I ever ate was in Venice. I was raised in New Jersey which is known for their tomatoes, but the ones in Italy are so good, I eat them like apples. There is nothing more refreshing than a slice of watermelon on a hot summer day, although I still can't get used to watching the Italians eat watermelon with a knife and fork.

The fruit stands in Italy exhibit their produce the way a clothing boutique displays its clothes. The fruit stand vendors take a lot of pride in their products. It took us a few shopping trips to learn that in Italy, you don't select your own fruit and vegetables. It's customary for the merchant to choose them for you. We were used to picking, squeezing, and smelling our fruit before we purchased it. We learned to trust these fruit vendors after we stubbornly told one that we wanted the big green figs. He suggested we buy the over-ripened black ones. I thought he was trying to get rid of the rotten ones, passing them on to unsuspecting American tourists, so we decided to take both. The green were good; however, the black figs were amazing. It is now our ritual that when we start a day tour, we buy a few bags of fruit for the day, and we always trust that the vendor is going to give us his best.

Albergo Terminus

Owner: Antonello Passera / General Manager: Christina Zucchi
Lungo Lario Trieste, 14-22100 / Como, Italy
Telephone: ++39031329111 / Fax: ++39031302550
E-Mail: info@albergoterminus.it / Web: www.albergoterminus.com

★★★★ **Price guide:** €135–€155/single, €156–€236/double • Major credit cards accepted **Amenities:** Air conditioning • Bar • Cable/Satellite TV • Internet • Airport: Milan • Nearby towns: Como, Milan • Restaurant: Breakfast €16, lunch & dinner à la carte • Total rooms: 40 **Activities:** Boat rental • Dock on lake • Fishing • Golf • Gym • Massage • Sauna • Shopping: silk and leather • Water skiing **Additional Information:** Small meeting facility: 12 people • Extra bed: €20 • Parking: €17

In 1930, Albergo Terminus opened under the management of the same family who owns and operates it today. It closed in 1988 for a renovation that would preserve this 20th century building in its original liberty style. Albergo Terminus reopened at the end of 1994 with an understated elegance characteristic of the finest Lombardy taste.

After countless excursions to the Como region, we suggest you stay at Albergo Terminus for it combines an incomparable location in the heart of Como, the silk capital of Italy, with unsurpassed sweeping views over the waters of the lake. The Bar della Terme, a café restaurant, offers your family the ability to sit outdoors on the terrace while enjoying the visions that surround you. Just a few steps from the hotel gates are the boat docks. Lake boats and ferries are the customary method of transportation, a great way for kids and seniors alike to cover a lot of territory in an unimposing yet amusing style. You will pass lakeside villages, hotels, and villas with their elaborate waterfront gardens.

Lake Como has the only school in Europe that administers licenses for seaplane pilots. To appreciate the panorama from above, you need not be a daring aviator. A railway from Como will take you straight up 713 meters to Brunate, or you can experience the cable car ride from Argegno to Pigra. Lake Como, with its close proximity to Milan, offers Italian fashion apparel, leather goods, local artistry, and unique handicrafts. Many restaurants abound at this location. One morning, since breakfast was not included in our room price, David and I enjoyed a cappuccino and croissant at a local café bar while the boys ventured across the cathedral square for an American fix of McDonald's.

Two years ago fortune came upon us when the Barroni family moved up the street from our home here in Atlanta. Natives of the Lombardi region, they make regular retreats to their bequested home above Como in the town of Lemna. The opportunity for our families to be together in Italy was an added delight. Experiencing a country from the vantage of people indigenous to the area will impart a unique perspective. Daniella and Bepe (Joe) have three sons, Alessandro who is twenty-four, Flippo who is twenty, and Edwardo who is ten. While David, Isaac, Jacob, and I stayed at the hotel, Ari had the rare adventure of sleeping over his friend's house in another country. We joined together each day for sight-seeing and culinary pleasures. Joe's and Daniella's mother, Pinuccia, took pride in teaching me the traditional method of preparing Polenta with delicious sauces made of either vegetables or meat gravy called Polenta e Puccia.

Albergo Terminus has forty rooms, a large suite, and a romantic room in the "Tower" popular with honeymooning couples. All rooms are well equipped with air conditioning, mini-bar, TV, modern modem service, hair dryers, and sound-proofed doors and windows. Albergo Terminus does not have a swimming pool; however, sports such as water skiing, rowing, tennis, and many golf clubs including the famous and exclusive Hotel Villa D'Este are nearby. We had two rooms connected by a private foyer and hallway entrance, giving rise to quiet moments for all.

Cardano Hotel

Director: Patrizio Strino
Malpensa International Airport / Via al Campo, 10 / 21010 Cardano al Campo (Va) / Italy
Telephone: ++390331261011262163 / Fax: ++390331730829
E-Mail: info@cardanohotel.com / Web: www.cardanohotel.com

★★★★ **Price guide:** €119–€144 • Major credit cards accepted **Amenities:** Air conditioning • Bar • Cable/Satellite TV • Internet • Nearby airport: Milan • Nearby towns: Como, Milan • Meal included: Breakfast, no restaurant • Total rooms: 40 **Activities:** • Swimming pool **Additional Information:** • Free shuttle service hotel/airport, 6:30 a.m. to 11:00 a.m. • Additional bed: €31

We desired a location to permit us to roll out of bed, eat breakfast, and arrive promptly for our flight back to the states. The Cardano Hotel is just a few minutes by car from Milan's Malpensa Airport.

This recently built, modern facility has an architectural style reminiscent of a miniature coliseum. This is a modest facility with all the amenities necessary for a convenient airport stay. Its rooms provide the necessary rest, and all are equipped with air-conditioning, color TV, radio, mini-bar, and telephone. If time permits, the kids can enjoy one last swim in the pool before enduring their extended flight home.

We arrived from Lago di Como late in the evening. While the boys were unwinding in front of the TV, David and I took a five-minute ride down the road to get pizza-to-go for dinner. The Nelbuco del Mulo's restaurant's brick oven pies cooked by Marco were exceptional. The opportunity to be in his company added to the pleasure of the evening - true Italian hospitality. As we lingered in anticipation of our food, he was resolute in gratuitously introducing us to his favorite local wines.

Hotel Villa Malpensa

Owner: Fausto Bonini / Manager: Giuseppe Gemmo
Via Don Andrea Sacconago, 1 / 21010 Vizzola Ticino (VA) / Italy
"In front of Milano Malpensa Airport Terminal #1"
Telephone: ++39 0331 230944 / Fax: ++39 0331 230950
E-Mail: info@hotelvillamalpensa.com / Web: www.hotelvillamalpensa.com

★★★★ **Price Guide:** €170–€260 • Major Credit Cards accepted **Amenities:** Air conditioning • Bar • TV • Internet • Nearby airports are Milan and Malpensa • Nearest town is Milan, Vizzola Ticino • Restaurant. Breakfast is included. • Total number of rooms - 65 **Activities:** In nearby Parco Delchino: golf, tennis, biking, and jogging • Shopping for Milan's high fashion • Swimming pool **Additional Information:** Free parking • Conference Center • Airport shuttle, eight hundred meters from the Airport of Malpensa

How unexpected! An enchanting early 20th century villa, only eight hundred meters from the Milano Malpensa International Airport! Villa Malpensa is situated in the center of the Ticino National Park and the medieval village of Vizzola Ticino. Completely restored in 1991, Villa Malpensa was originally the old central rail station of Milan as well as the opulent residence of Count Caproni. This dignified liberty style villa with its patio entrance and side verandahs is rich in style and comfort. The hotel's sixty-five bedrooms, including eight superior rooms and one suite, are more than ideal considering the Villa's

close proximity to the airport. The rooms all contain the essential modern comforts of satellite TV, mini bar, direct telephone line with modem connection, air conditioning, hair dryer, and safe. Some rooms have balconies and overlook the Ticino valley.

Hotel Villa Malpensa's strategic location to Malpensa airport, combined with its old-world charm, is suitable for both business and pleasure. Dine in their fine restaurant, which features both Italian and international cuisine, or arrange festive dinner receptions in the Salone degli Affreschi where "Italian royals" once awaited their trains.

Ansitz Heufler

Schlosshotel - Restaurant / Familie Steiner
Oberrasen 37 / I-39030 Rasen im Antholzertal
Tel. 0039/0474/498582 / Fax 0039/0474/498046
E-Mail: info@heufler.com / Web: www.heufler.com

★★★ **Price Guide:** €104–€144/double, plus €30 high season **Amenities:** Bar • Airports: Bolzano, Verona, Venice, Munich, Innsbruck, & Zurich • Nearby towns: Bressanone/Brixen, Kronplatz and Olang Valdaora • Restaurant: Breakfast included; dinner à la carte • Total rooms: 13 **Activities:** Biking • Children's park • Golf: 40 km • Gym: nearby • Hiking • Horseback riding • Massage: nearby • Sauna: nearby • Shopping • Skiing • Swimming pool: nearby • Tennis courts: nearby • Cultural tours **Additional Information:** Guided wine tasting • Tour of the Dolomites • Typical Torggelen • Additional bed: €24 • Restaurant: closed Tuesdays; open for lunch July & August, December & January • Half board: €26

Come and visit with the Steiner family on the Heufler estate, whose caring and warmth add much to this already special little castle. Built over 425 years ago by the Heufler dynasty of Hohenbuhel, it holds a very important position in Tyrollean history. The *Hearnstube* is one of the most valuable and significant renaissance *parlours* (sitting rooms) in this entire Alpine region. Its warm and friendly surroundings are pleasant to gather with family and friends.

Thomas Steiner is a remarkable, well-educated, young proprietor. During the day he is on top of every detail with a genuineness that fills the rooms. By night, he is the *sommelier* (wine server) for the hotel's outstanding intimate restaurant. When it comes to wine, order your meal and leave the rest up to him. He stocks 140 different labels. Although Thomas is the only one fluent in English in the establishment, each staff person goes out of their way to assure that your needs are met. Michl Steiner, his brother, is the *chef d' cuisine*.

As in all our recommended places to stay and dine, the kitchen was sensitive to our children's American palates. Johanna, their mother, will greet you each morning with a full breakfast which is available from 7:30 a.m. until 12:00 noon. Your kids can choose from eggs, bacon, cheese, breads, and *musli*, (a fresh made cereal) with yogurt, bananas, and apples. The first night our boys were extremely jet-lagged, having driven all day and just arrived in Roma. They went with their stand-by of *pasta pomodori* (pasta with tomato sauce). We have a house rule, "You don't have to eat it but trying it is a must." Michl's style of cooking is so original that with each taste, the kids were inspired to venture further. Jacob and Ari loved *la crema di zucca con panna acida* (the pumpkin soup with crème) and *il petto affumicato d' anatra su cavolo blu e filetti d' agrumi* (breast of duck with blue cauliflower and slices of citrus). Isaac's X-game style of snowboarding had him craving a hardier *l' agnello brasato su crauti stufati e patate al forno* (grilled lamb with sour kraut and oven baked potatoes). The pumpkin soup still has me longing for more. When I asked Michl his ingredients for this mousse-like soup, he was quick to inform me that the most important ingredient is that, "Everything is prepared from the heart." However, we all agreed that a stay at Ansitz Heufler is incomplete without *il tortino di cioccolato, gelato alla lavenda e mirtilli rossi* (the most delectable chocolate cake with lavender ice cream) for a most sensual sweet experience.

Ansitz Heufler's accommodations are ideal for families. They have five rooms and four suites. Our favorite was the Heufler Suite Number 8 which we resided in during our stay. Ansitz Heufler can organize many activities for you and your family including guided mountain and skiing treks through the Dolomites. Cycling, tennis, or the opportunity to relax at the spa of a partner hotel can also be arranged. For a unique experience, Thomas Steiner will take you on a guided wine tasting along the countryside. Kronplatz is one of the region's largest and most modern ski resorts. This pristine and nearly treeless skier's paradise has a total of 85 kilometers of downhill runs fit for all levels of ability. The long and expansive Olang slope is especially suitable for families. There are natural toboggan runs throughout the area and 280 kilometers of cross-country ski trails. As for us, this little castle was a warm welcome after an invigorating day on the panoramic slopes of Kronplatz, Plan de Corones.

Hotel Elephant

Owner: Family Falk/Heiss / General Manager: Elisabeth Heiss & Heinrich Radmuller
I-39042 Bressanone/Brixen / Via Rio Bianco, 4 WeiBlahnstr. / Italy
Telephone: ++39 0472 832 750 / Fax: ++39 0472 836 579
E-Mail: elephant.brixen@acs.it / Website: www.hotelelephant.com

★★★★ **Price Guide:** €192-€243, children 0-11 years are free in parents room • Major Credit Cards accepted **Amenities:** Air conditioning • Babysitting by request • Bar • Cable/satellite TV • Internet • Laundry • Airport: Bolzano, Bressanone/Brixen • Nearby towns: Bressanone/Brixen, Bolzano • Restaurant: Breakfast included, Lunch & dinner à la carte; half board: €30; full board; €51 • Total rooms: 44 & suites; total beds: 72 beds **Activities:** Biking • Children's park • Golf: 50 km • Gym • Hiking • Massage • Sauna • Shopping • Skiing • Swimming pool • Tennis court **Additional Information:** Solarium, museum quality painting and antiques • Many nearby children's parks • The price guide for the high season of the Junior Suite with full board: €347 • Meeting facilities • Open from March 15th - November 4th and from December 6th- January 6th. • Half board/full board

In the 16th century, King John III of Portugal had an elephant sent from Goa by ship to Genoa. This was a gift for Emperor Archduke Maximilian of Austria. By the time the elephant reached Brixen, it was quite in need of rest. The only stable in town belonged to the inn outside the walls. During the two weeks during the winter of 1550 to 1551 that this noble elephant spent here, people came from distant regions to view this important and prodigious guest. The innkeeper, realizing his unanticipated notoriety, commissioned an extensive fresco of his biggest guest to be portrayed on the street wall, renaming the hotel and transforming its destiny forever.

Hotel Elephant has continued to thrive under the direct descendants of its pachyderm days. Wolfgang Heiss was born here in 1923, and he was raised at Hotel Elephant. A bright, proud, and humorous man of seventy-eight, he contentedly sits each afternoon at a booth in the reception area, surrounded by the heritage that has been generated throughout the centuries at the resort. Behind him rests the pictures of his great, great, great-grandfather, Romanus Mayr, 1755 to 1845, and great, great, great-grandmother, Maria Mayr, 1744 to 1814. As we speak, the sun illuminates a stained glass window, paying tribute to his great-grandfather, Postmeister Ferdinand Egarter, KK, who made the oldest stamp in the world. Wolfgang's deceased wife, Marianne Heiss, recognized the importance of documenting the days gone by. She organized the *Hausmuseum* (house museum), an important collection of objects depicting Hotel Elephant's significant place in time.

Family lineage extends far beyond the Heiss ancestry at Hotel Elephant. For centuries, families have vacationed here, and grown children return with their own children. A story was recounted to me about a young couple who came every Easter, October and Christmas. After many years of marriage, they gave birth to twins and telephoned Marianne to inform her that they could no longer handle such a trip. She insisted they must come to Hotel Elephant with the babies. Marianne enlisted her children, Elisabeth and her sister Claudia, to baby-sit the entire week, while the twosome enjoyed the holiday in their accustomed carefree style. The man is now the godfather to Elisabeth's son, Michael. The twins are thirty years old and have continued to stay at the Hotel Elephant over the past three decades.

The employees of Hotel Elephant have the same allegiance as the guests. Heinrich Radmüeller, the Director, Alfred Aschbacher, the Porter, and Sergio Fiaschi, the restaurant *maître d'* have all remained here over thirty years. Fabio, a four-year employee, speaks seven different languages and is often at reception to assure your holiday success. During Christmas, I took notice of him calling previous guests throughout Europe to wish them well for the coming year.

Upon arrival in our rooms, we were wel-

comed *Con i complimenti* (with compliments) by a basket of fruit, nuts, and fresh baked cookies that was continually replenished each day. The note that accompanied the gift expressed, "Welcome. We wish you a pleasant stay. Elisabeth Heiss with family and the Elephant team."

As Elisabeth moves about, she conveys the tradition of the past with unobstructed visions of Hotel Elephant's flourishing future. Nonchalantly, she in conjunction with their personnel, bring into being an ambiance that encourages your family to "live like it is your own home." Royalty have done just that for centuries. The green hall on the second level has a special dining area adjacent to their rooms for these imperial guests. When these sovereign personalities visit, they may choose to be isolated from the rest of the hotel. There are a total of forty-four rooms and seventy-two beds, all of them unique in their décor, ranging from standard and deluxe to junior suites. All rooms have television and some have balconies. There are several possibilities for adjoining rooms, which Elisabeth tells me is ideal for families and popular with couples that have snoring problems. I particularly liked our accommodations which were across the street. This part of the hotel is nestled in a park with a swimming pool and lawn, perfect for an afternoon siesta. The lower level was complete with a small workout room, sauna, steam, Turkish bath, and a tanning room. Each morning, I drifted down the stairs and exercised just long enough for the spas to heat up. David and the boys found its warmth and relaxation gratifying after a day of competitive skiing on the mountain. Massages are available by appointment. All rooms are equipped with a private bath and phone, and some have a television and a balcony.

The hotel boasts three separate dining rooms: the Altdeutsche Stuben, Apostelstube, and the Zirbelstube. All elicit a traditional old-world allure presenting the ideal backdrop for a superb dining experience. For a true delicacy, request the *Anatra* (duck). Their Lobster Ravioli, deep colored pasta filled with lobster and twisted at either end, is similar to a fine piece of candy and it remains vivid in my mind. Pleasing the kid's palates was effortless with creamed vegetable soup, grilled steak, pasta, and *Pommes frites* (French fries). Sergio is always on hand to match the perfect wine to your taste and cuisine.

Hotel Elephant is situated on the outskirts of Bressanone or Brixen, depending on the ancestry of the person to whom you are speaking. This region has been disputed over for centuries, and in 1972 the "Autonomy Package" became part of the Italian Constitution. This is when the German language was officially reintroduced and earned equal status with Italian. Hence, two names for every town.

Bressanone, filled with chic boutiques and old-world architecture, gives rise to extensive natural landscapes with an array of outdoor recreation. They range from relaxing family walks along mountain roads past farmsteads and guesthouses to challenging alpine excursions. While staying in Bressanone, we continued to ski Kronplatz located only 60 kilometers away; however, there is an enormous range of winter sports centers throughout Tyrol and close to Hotel Elephant. Dolomiti ski passes make it possible to ski on several mountains during one holiday. Eisacktal Valley is above Bressanone and has two ski centers, Gitschberg/Jochtal and Plose. In this area is the nine-kilometer Trametsch downhill run, South Tyrol's longest.

We are fortunate that the saga of the elephant did not end in 1551 but carries on to the present day, as the opportunity to stay at one of Italy's foremost hotels in this most picturesque northern village is a true delight.

Isaac Soars

I had an adventure flying to Italy one time that should not be recreated. Our flight took us from Atlanta, Georgia to Zurich, Switzerland and then from Switzerland to Venice, Italy. On the long plane ride, I told my Mom that I was not feeling well. She told me to lie down, and I would feel much better. So, that is exactly what I did, but soon I was up again and running to the bathroom at the back of the plane.

For the next two hours, I was sick to my stomach. Finally, the flight attendant let my Mom and I go to the first class where there were beds and much more room. When we arrived in Zurich, all I could do was rest on a bench. When it was time to board the plane for Italy, my Dad had to pick me up because I was too tired and had difficulty walking. Luckily, I slept through the whole flight and when we arrived in Italy, I felt perfectly healthy.

The first hotel we stayed in was called Villa Luppis (Northern Italy). The hotel was warm and cozy. Someone was always offering to help us. This villa was a great home on a large estate. The villa was very clean and had a pool in the back of the house. If we woke early in the morning, which I did because of the time difference, I could see the sun come up over the mountains. In the morning, we were served a breakfast of eggs and a variety of fruits, cereals, and yogurt. Staying in a villa makes you experience life as an Italian.

Ciao (bye), Isaac Levinson

Debra's Note

I found it interesting to read Isaac's account of his in-flight ailment. The way I remember it, David and I spent nine grueling hours racing him to the rest room and cleaning the area with towels and disinfectant handed to us by a somewhat distraught flight attendant. It took a lot of pleading with the flight attendant to get us moved to first class, which happened to be completely vacant. Finally, we received the attention we needed—hot towels for Isaac and hot espresso for me.

Our first flight to Rome with the boys was a complete disaster. Isaac fell asleep on the floor in the bulkhead area and managed to get kicked in the eye by a passing flight attendant. Ari spilled his drink all over himself and was soaking wet. Jacob woke in the middle of the flight holding his throat with pain. We soothed Isaac's black eye, changed Ari's drenched clothes and gave Jacob homeopathic remedies and tea.

The lesson I learned is that, as parents, we have to be advocates for our kids on the ground and in the air, and we have to be prepared to handle just about anything. By the time you are ready to explore the Roman Empire, you will feel that you have already conquered it.

Parkhotel Laurin

Owner: Franz Joseph Staffler / (3rd Generation Proprietor) / Manager: M. J. Remigius Havlik
Via Laurin 4 / 1-39100 Bolzano-Bozen / Italy
Telephone: ++390471311000 / Fax: ++390471311148
E-Mail: mailto:info@laurin.it / Website: www.laurin.it

★★★★ **Price guide:** €158-€260 • Major credit cards accepted **Amenities:** Air conditioning • Babysitting on request • Bar • Cable/Satellite TV • Internet • Laundry • Airport: Bolzano • Nearby towns: Bolzano, Bressanone/ Brixen, Merano • Restaurant: Breakfast included; lunch & dinner additional €22-€40 • Total rooms: 96; including 10 Junior suites **Activities:** Biking • Children's park • Golf: 25 km • Hiking • Horseback riding • Shopping: clothes, leather and knives • Skiing: nearby • Swimming pool **Additional Information:** Open all year • Meeting facility • Piano music and jazz performances • Half board/full board

Anything magical should begin with a fairy tale. So it is for Parkhotel Laurin with its name derived from a king whose legend is told in South Tyrol's most incredible tale. Once upon a time, high among the gray rocks of the Dolomites that overshadow the scenery to the west of Bolzano, was a rose garden that glowed at dusk. It belonged to the dwarf king Laurin who fell so desperately in love with a princess named Similde that he abducted her. When her father's knights came to save Similde, Laurin hid in the garden. The movement of the roses revealed his location. He said, "These roses betrayed me. If the knights hadn't seen them, they would have never come up on my mountain." Angered over this sudden change of fate, he put a curse on the rose garden: "Neither by day nor by night should human eyes ever again behold its beauty." Nevertheless, he forgot dusk, which is why we can still see the crimson glow of the rose garden as the final rays of sunshine on it just before the day's end.

Approaching the center of Bolzano, we were awestruck by the magnificence of such a grand hotel in a private park, in the middle of town. A step inside this modern European hotel reveals a harmonious blend of traditions and up to the minute renovations. The Parkhotel Laurin is still owned by the Staffler family who constructed it in 1909.

Prior to World War II, in the 1930's, famous and noble people frequented the hotel. In 1937, Victtorio Emanuele III, King of Italy, rendezvoused here with Mussolini over dinner. Since that time, it has become a favorite place to stay for business and pleasure. Mr. Havlik's contagious love of Parkhotel Laurin is enthralling. As a general manager, he creates an atmosphere that invites your family to relax while taking full advantage of the hotel's exquisite park, playgrounds, swimming pool, and outdoor restaurant called Belle Epoque. Their children's menu, Il Piccolo, offers kid friendly choices for the young ones.

Parkhotel Laurin's lawns, gardens, and shady paths are the gateway to the Dolomites inimitable shopping, sports, and sightseeing. The Lorenzi Brothers, located on the Goethe-Strasse offer two thousand different knives and more than two hundred diverse types of scissors and custom made hunting knives designed by Silvano Lorenzi. Essentially, any type of cutting instrument with a blade can be obtained here. I purchased a long sought after mandolin for precision cut cheese, fruit, and vegetables. Jacob found an L'orologeria, (watchmaker) who repaired an heirloom piece from his grandfather, complete with a new leather band.

Visit Runkelstein castle, Lake Carezza, and Bolzano's seven high profile museums. Don't miss the Bolzano Archaeological Museum where people from all over the world swarm to see the naturally mummified remains of "Oetzi" who has been kept preserved in eternal ice for over 5,300 years. My kids were mesmerized, although Ari felt his appearance necessitated a cosmetic makeover. Oetzi was

discovered in September of 1991 by a German couple, Mr. and Mrs. Simon, when a glacier began to melt, and it released him. He was a bronze-age hunter, and his remains gave clues to life during that time. The museum presents the story in a sequential manner. Headphones are available in many languages including English.

For lunch, the boys voted, hands down, for Restaurant Pizzeria NuBbaumer, owned and operated by the Plattner family. This is a popular spot for local Tyrolleans, and they come in droves to devour their sensational pizzas. They have a full menu but the pies are the *la piece de résistance*. They are located at Via Bottai 11, and the telephone number is ++390471-973950.

During the seven years of renovation, Franz Joseph Staffler acquired original works of art from the 1900's to the present. Something that has always bothered him is the use of framed pages from calendars, reproductions of prints, and other valueless pictures placed on hotel walls. Instead, each hotel room has its own unique painting. Upon arrival, you will be given a short history lesson about the artwork. The marble bathrooms lend an air of elegance. The Laurin Bar with its frescoed, carved wooden ceilings and columns was our favorite place to sit and unwind. Each Friday night they feature "All That Jazz" with a variety of local musicians.

Pension Maximilian

Owner & Manager: George and Gertrud Holzer
Via Kerla Str. 4 / I-39030 Olang-Valdaora / Bolzano, Italy
Telephone: ++390474496227 / Fax: ++390474495644
E-Mail: info@pension-maximillian.com / Web: www.pension-maximillian.com

★★★ **Price Guide:** €36–€56 per person/per night; includes breakfast and dinner • Major credit cards accepted
Amenities: Bar • Cable/Satellite TV • Restaurant: guests only • Airports: Bolzano, Innsbruck and Verona •
Restaurant: guests only • Total rooms: 12 **Activities:** Biking • Golf: driving range: 1 km. • Hiking • Horseback riding
• Massage: nearby • Sauna: nearby • Skiing: nearby • Tours of the Dolomites

Walking through the small elegant town of Olang-Valdaora, we came upon this gem. A real find for a family looking for a pleasant, unassuming family-run hotel near the exceptional ski resort of Kronplatz. The *pension* (rates include bed, breakfast, & dinner) has twelve simple rooms, all with private bathrooms. The ground floor contains a sauna and tanning bed for your après ski pleasure. On the main level, the dining room and a cozy bar with fireplace offers warmth from the cold winter nights.

Originally built as a bed and breakfast in 1964 by Gertrud and Maximilian Holzer, the Pension was renovated and enlarged in 1980. Today, George and his mother Gertrud see to the needs of their guests.

A pre-fixed menu, included with your reasonably priced half board, always consists of fresh ingredients. The food, which is an intermingling of many regions, is served family style and is all prepared by Gertrud and George; a plentiful salad bar, warm bread, hearty soup, traditional meats and delicate raviolis that will melt in your mouth are just a sampling of their varying menu.

A short 80 kilometer walk from the hotel door and you are on the bus heading towards the *pistas* (slopes). The boys met up with other kids and confidently headed to the mountain ahead of us. George speaks excellent English and is always available to give you tips on skiing and snowboarding, in particular. His friends opened the Ski-Snowboard School Cima. We found the instruction and organization superb. They offer a complete range of winter activities. A full day beginners ski school for the kids at Kronplatz costs € 155-€ 185 for five or six days. They will entertain your children from 10:00 a.m. to 3:00 p.m. This includes two, three-hour skiing or snow boarding lessons accompanied by lunch, followed by additional skiing or the opportunity to play. During a one-hour lesson, Ari progressed from snowplow to near parallel skiing. School Cima is about "fun for kids." For adults, instructors offer lessons for beginners, advanced skiers, snow boarders, carving, telemark skiing, or racing. Contact Cima School at www.cimaschool.com, telephone: ++39 0474 497216 or fax: ++39 0474 495700.

Gertrude and George are anxious for your family to visit their petite chalet set amongst splendid mountains, amidst a scenic town. Their accommodations are modest however the food and service are reassuring of a hassle free holiday.

Pension Stefaner

Owner: Family Villgrattner / Manager: Georg and Mathilde
1-39050 St. Zyprian-Tiers / Dolomites – South Tyrol / Italy
Telephone: ++390471642175 / Fax: ++390471-642302
E-Mail: info@stefaner.com / Web: www.stefaner.com

★★★ **Price Guide:** €39-€53 per person, per day **Amenities:** Bar • Airport: Bolzano • Nearby town: Bolzano • Restaurant: Breakfast & dinner included; hotel guest only • Activities: hiking **Additional Information:** Children under 3 years: free in parent's room • Children 4 -15 years: 10 to 70% discount • Half board available for stays of three days or more

Nestled amidst one of Europe's largest ranges of high alpine meadowland is the Pension Stefaner. *Pension* rates include bed, breakfast, & dinner. Mathilde, Georg, and their children greet you with authentic *Tyrolean* (regional) hospitality. They are delighted to welcome guests into their chalet to simply relax among some of the world's most amazing mountain scenery. The rooms are simple and clean, suggestive of a mountain cottage

This region is a genuine paradise for mountain walkers, hikers, and bikers with over 300 kilometers of trails, wonderful air, and plenty of sunshine. When winter arrives, this entire area transforms into a glimmering white landscape with over 70 kilometers of downhill ski runs and cross-country trails. Mathilde will organize special skiing weeks and winter excursions for your family; however, she believes that the area has more to offer in the summer months when journeying with young children.

Georg Villgrattner is most often seen with his apron and white chef's hat. He exemplifies the proverb, "The way to a man's heart is through his stomach" quite literally. Each night, he prepares a menu of prearranged fresh seasonal fare. It has been said that many of their guests return to Pension Stefaner especially for his good food.

Mithilda is so eager to accommodate your family. Although Pension Stefaner is diminutive in size, the warmth of the Villgrattner family presents the kind of hospitality only found in this style of lodging.

Villa Luppis

Owner: Dott. Giorgio & Stefania Ricci Luppis
33080 Rivarotta di Pasiano (PN) / Via S. Martino, 34 / Italy
Telephone: ++390434626969 / Fax: ++390434626228
E-Mail: hotel@villaluppis.it / Web: www.villaluppis.it

★★★★ **Price guide:** €180–€298 • Major credit cards accepted **Amenities:** Air conditioning • Baby sitting • Bar • Cable/satellite TV • Airport: Venice • Nearby towns: Venice, Pordenone, Oderzo and Trieste • Restaurant: Breakfast included; lunch & dinner à la carte • Total rooms: 31; 4 suites **Activities:** • Biking • Golf: nearby • Gym • Shopping: nearby • Skiing: Cortina d' Ampezzo • Swimming pool • Tennis courts • Cultural tours arranged **Additional Information:** • Half board/full board • Wine tasting classes • Cooking school • Photo safari in naturalistic oasis • Meeting facilities

Villa Luppis was originally an old Camaldolite monastery called "San Martino Ripea Ruptae." The monastery was damaged during the war between the Republic of Venice and the house of Hapsburgs in the 1500's. In the 1800's, the Chiozza-Luppis family acquired it. The family turned it into a superb country house and elegant estate, where they carried out public relations for their industrial and diplomatic activities.

Today, the villa still recalls the splendor of the past thanks to its refined quality and careful renovations. When the Luppis family opened the villa to guests in 1993, they were committed to maintaining the feel of the original home. The entrance hall opens to an arch that frames a view of the park, where there is a large *terrazzo* (terrace) before the main door.

Each of the six suites is decorated in a unique style, some designed with families in mind while others provide privacy for a romantic interlude. Our favorite is the opulent "La Suite Rosa" with its Louis XVI style furniture, French fresco, antique mirror, and balcony overlooking the park. In addition to the suites, there are twenty-seven bedrooms, all with distinctive décor, air-conditioning, television, stereo, and bar service from the refrigerator.

Villa Luppis is also home to Giorgio's and Stefania's young daughter, Beatrice, so the hosts are very aware of the needs of young families.

Babysitting arrangements can be made when requested in advance of your stay. Outside the villa doors are five *hectares* of grounds with a swimming pool, tennis courts, bicycles for touring the surrounding park, and shuttle service to and from Venice. The property has special agreements that allow you to visit a top designer fashion outlet and nearby golf complexes. They can arrange itineraries through Venetian villas and Friuli castles. Marco Polo airport in Venice is 50 kilometers away, and transportation can be arranged for an additional fee. Then there's the food!

The gourmet dining room features frescoed walls, art objects, period furnishings, and live music in the background. The best part is the authentic regional specialties served here, complete with local wines, including their own private label which magnificently accompanies each course. Chef Antonio Sanna was quite accommo-dating to the varied preferences of our three sons. The meal flowed like a great novel, with each chapter of courses leaving you yearning for the next.

If you dream of cooking these gastronomic masterpieces yourself, Stefania Ricca Luppis will delight in arranging a one-to-five day cooking school. She and her staff will create a unique course for you, with a minimum of eight people in attendance. Inform them what you are interested in learning, and they will handle the details. The classes include visits to local markets and cheese producers. A wine tasting can be included as part of your program or can be enjoyed on a separate day. The price varies, depending on your course curriculum.

At Villa Luppis, you will be surrounded by exceptional charm, with the kind of hospitality typical of a first-class hotel. Your family will love the relaxed, friendly service in this elegant atmosphere.

Hotel Ancora

Owners/Directors: Flavia and Renato Sartor / Reservations: Mrs. Assunta
Corso Italia, 62 / 32043 Cortina d'Ampezzo (BL) / Italy
Telephone: ++3904363261 / Fax: ++3904363265
E-Mail: info@hotelancoracortino.com / Web: www.hotelancoracortina.com

★★★★ **Price guide:** €118–€176 per person/per day sharing a double room with half board including breakfast, dinner, taxes and service **Amenities:** Air conditioning • Baby sitting: by request • Bar • Cable/Satellite TV • Internet • Laundry • Restaurant: Breakfast & dinner included; lunch: €37 or à la carte • Total rooms: 49 **Activities:** • Biking • Fishing: summer in nearby Lakes of Gheding, Pianozes, Scin and Boite River. • Golf: 1km • Gym • Hiking • Horseback riding • Massage • Sauna • Shopping: jewelry, antiques, high fashion, wine shops and carpets. • Skiing • Cultural tours **Additional Information:** • Gambero Rosso Editore awarded Hotel Ancora for the third time, as one of the best eleven hotels in Italy for quality, comfort and cuisine. • Half board/full board

A stay in Hotel Ancora was unavailable during our visit to the area; however, through much correspondence, I developed a special, warm sentiment for Mrs. Assunta who graciously opened her hotel doors to us on three separate occasions. Initially, she insisted that upon arriving in town, we should come and enjoy an *aperitif* at the hotel's Terrazza Viennese bar with terrace lounge. This is the central meeting place on the famous *Corso Italia* for influential people the world over. On a subsequent visit, Mrs. Assunta personally guided me through the Ancora's exquisite suites and stunning bedrooms. The tour left me yearning to linger. The third call was the charm—the international cuisine and fine dining experience of Ristorante Petit Fleur. The meal was outstanding from beginning to end. The service was attentive yet discreet. Their personal label wine is not to be overlooked. It is understandable why Hotel Ancora holds the recognition of being one of the top eleven hotels in Italy for quality and price.

Though I did not have the chance to meet Flavia and Renato Sartor, their refined touch was ever present throughout Hotel Ancora's rooms that blend art, history, and their beloved antiques. Although they go out of their way with provisions for babies and young children, Mrs. Assunta recommends their hotel is best suited for children ten years and older.

Hotel Locanda San Barnaba

Owner/Manager: Silvia Okolicsanvi
Calle del Traghetto, 2785-2786 / Sestiere di Dorsoduro / Venezia, Italy
Telephone: ++390412411233 / Fax: +39-041-2413812
Mobile Telephone: ++3903487939603 / E-Mail: info@locanda-sanbarnaba.com
Website: http://www.locanda-sanbarnaba.com/

★★★ **Price Guide:** €120-€210 • Major credit cards accepted **Amenities:** Air conditioning • Baby sitting upon request • Bar • Cable/Satellite TV • Internet • Laundry • Airport: Venice • Nearby town: Venice • No restaurant • Breakfast included • Total rooms: 13; 2 junior suites, 2 superior doubles, 8 classics and 1 single **Activities:** • Boat rentals with drivers: Water Taxi, Gondola • Beach: 30 min. Isle di Lido • Shopping: Merano glass • Cultural tours: artistic walks

On this particular holiday, we flew straight into the Venice Airport. In the terminal, a tourist information booth awaits travelers, which we have found to provide reliable information throughout Italy. To discover new and unusual accommodations often requires us to journey without a prearranged booking. We were aptly guided to Hotel Locanda San Barnaba. They told us this 16th century palace had just opened after a decade of delicate restoration and is situated near many of Venice's notable places of interest. Jet lagged and tired after a long flight, we opted for their suggestion.

Leaving our suitcases in the car, taking only the essentials in our backpacks, we boarded the *Vaporetto linea n° 1* (water bus) to the Cá Rezzonico stop. A quick two minute walk via a few passageways, and we were affably greeted by Silvia, the successor of this Locanda which once belonged to her grandfather. The hotel's prospect of future success was immediately apparent. All the essential ingredients were present: Serene neighborhood, superb location, and modern amenities with architecture reminiscent of its period. Each one of the rooms at Locanda San Barnaba depicts a tale — the "Lover"s Nest," "The Artist Studio," "The Philosopher's Refuge," and the "Playwright's Chamber," where his muse is known to remain. Our room had a loft where the kids should have slept had they not been so jet-lagged. Unable to resist sleep upon arrival at 5:00 p.m., they were up all night watching TV, playing "GameBoy," and swimming in the oversized Jacuzzi tub. In the heat of summer, air conditioning is a welcome in each room. Enjoy the tranquility of the private garden alongside the Venetian canal as you eat breakfast or have an evening glass of *Prosecco* wine from the bar.

Taking a *passeggiata* (stroll) through the near byways, you will realize that you are well positioned in the center of Venice. Locanda San Barnaba is between Accademia Gallery, Piazza S. Marco, and the Rialto Bridge. One afternoon, wandering through a *piazza* (town square), we came upon an unusual wine shop. Large barrels of many regional wines lined this cavernous setting. The kids were as amused by the uniqueness as David and I. While the local Venetians brought in their bottles and chose their evening spirits, we too had to partake. We emptied our water bottles for the chance to experience this uncommon system of obtaining *vino*. With one red and one white in hand, all we were missing was the pizza. As the kids road their motorized scooters around us in the *piazza*, touching base for a slice of the divine, we sipped our select vintage.

Returning to the states, we were delighted to read *The New York Times* special travel section on Venice, which recommended Locanda San Barnaba. Stepping back in time through the doors of this palazzo sets the stage for discovering the fascination, beauty, and rhythm of Venice.

Owners: Menardi Family / Franca, Antonio, Alberta, and Andrea
Via Majon 110 / 32043 Cortina d'Ampezzo (Bl) / Italy
Telephone: 011390436-2400 / Fax: 011390436862183
E-Mail: info@hotelmenardi.it / Web: www.hotelmenardi.it

★★★ **Price Guide:** €55–€128, per person/per day with half board. • Major credit cards accepted **Amenities:** Bar • Cable/Satellite TV • Airport: Venice and Bolzano • Nearby towns: Belluno, Venice, and Cortina d' Ampezzo • Restaurant: Breakfast included; lunch & dinner are half board €20, full board €30 • Total rooms: 51 **Activities:** Biking • Fishing in the summer at a nearby lakes of Ghedina, Pianozes, Scin, and Boite River • Golf: 1 km • Hiking • Horseback riding • Shopping: jewelry, antiques, high fashion, wine shops and carpets. • Skiing **Additional information:** Special children's prices • Half board/full board

In 1836, the Menardi Müller family constructed the older main house for agricultural purposes. The strategic position of their home on the main carriageway linking the Italian Kingdom with the Hapsburg Empire influenced them to lease horses. There was an extreme need for the commercial wagons to tack on more horsepower, enabling them to make it up through the arduous Cimabanche Pass. At this point in time, part of the house became an Inn for the merchants traveling the Imperial Royal Street of Alemagne.

Luigi Menardi was the original proprietor of the hotel. In later years, he had the help of his son, Angelo, in converting the old farmhouse into the warm and cozy alpine inn that now exists. Angelo's wife and three sons, Antonio, Alberta, and Andrea are present today providing the same family touch and professional service their departed father and grandfather exhibited for over a century.

Hotel Menardi has a newer building sit-

ting adjacent to the park behind the original main house. The two lodges combined total fifty-one rooms, with six providing triple accommodations and five rooms are capable of connecting to one another.

The kids valued the hotel's collection of original work tools and remains of the craftsmanship of past generations. Together, we appreciated the intimacy of their hotel's unpretentious size and the wonderful family-style dining that is overseen with great regard, offering Italian and specialty local dishes, accompanied by an immense selection of some of the best Italian and foreign wines.

Il Fae'

Bed & Breakfast and more...
Owner: Sabina Valerio Brino Bet & Salvatore Valerio
Via Fae' 1-Borgo Frare / 31020 San. Pietro di Feletto (TV) / Italy
Telephone: ++390438-787117 / Fax: ++390438-787818
E-Mail: mail@ilfae.com / Web: www.ilfae.com

★★★ **Price Guide:** Bed & Breakfast: €78–€200/2-4 people per night in farmhouse; Villa rentals: €1100–€1600/8 people/week, €1800–€2400/11-12 people/week, final cleaning €15; Fae' Venice: €680–€780/week one bedroom apartment in Canareggio area of Venice **Amenities:** Laundry • Airport: Venice • Nearby towns: Asolo, Conegliano, Cortina d' Ampezzo, Treviso, and Vittorio Veneto • No restaurant • Breakfast included: dinner upon request: €30 **Activities:** Biking • Golf: 35 km at Cansiglio Golf Club • Hiking • Horseback riding • Shopping • Skiing • Swimming pool • Cultural tours **Additional Information:** Baby crib available • Classes Offered: 5 day cooking school €1300/person (4-8 people) all comprehensive, daily rates available, painting, and Italian language • Winery tours • Il fae has handmade products and produce

The advertisement in the magazine of La Cucina Italiana reads "Il Fae', Bed and Breakfast and more."Il Fae' is a gem of a location in the beautiful hills of San Pietro. Situated in the Northeast of Italy, it allows for easy access to Venice, Treviso, Asolo, Vittorio, Veneta, and the Dolomites. Since 1955, Sabina's grandfather, and then her father, owned this farmhouse. Through their careful renovations, they have created a rustic and homey ambiance.

As we approached Il Fae's peaceful countryside and farmhouse, we were enthusiastically greeted by Sabina, Salvatore, and their two teenage boys, Niccolo and Giuseppe. They are

there to ensure the success of your family's stay. It is not unusual for them to invite your family into their adjacent home to share a bottle of their own vineyard's personal labeled *Prosecco* wine. Being with Sabina and Salvatore was like staying with relatives who were so excited to share the richness of their culture and country. They took pride in showing us their town of Conegliano, which dates back 6000 years to the Neolithic Age. Walking about the town, you will see the ancient castle Torre della Guardia, a Jewish cemetery, the Duomo Sala Dei Battuti with its original frescoed façade, and paintings by Cima that depict the beauty of the surrounding hills.

You will enjoy the fresh bouquet of its wines along with the typical local gastronomy. We sampled some Venetian red wines at the oldest *Osteria* (bar) called Osteria Al Ponte where a glass of wine is referred to as an *Ombra* (shadow). Centuries ago, the farmers would come in from the fields of heat and take refuge in the shadows of the church walls. They would sit and drink vina rossa. Two wines that I would suggest are Donna Caterina a Raboso Veneto and Cecchetto Raboso 1997.

You can spend two or three days exploring the cities that surround Il Fae'. Treviso is a grand old city built at the concourse of the Sile and Bottenigo Rivers. The Bottenigo River then splits to form an enchanting array of glistening canals, which traverse through the houses and water the cities many flowering gardens. Vittorio Veneto owes its subsistance to the merging of two old towns. In the north, Serravalle contains the remains of the 'wall sand towers' built in the medieval times as a defense against invading Barbarians. To the south, Ceneda reaches on to the plain and is partially built on the surrounding hills.

Il Fae' offers cooking and Italian courses, painting classes, and winery tours of nearby vineyards. Guided excursions to Venice and special golf packages are available; therefore, while I prepare *Zuppa di Pesce*, a Venetian soup in the *limonaia* (original lemon plant storage), David and the boys may be off enjoying one of three nearby golf centers, biking, hiking, or riding trails. Later, we can all meet for a swim in their private pool.

Sabina remarks, "Staying in this particular atmosphere, you can learn many aspects of Italian cooking during their five-day course." Their chef is previously from the Hotel Ancora, a favorite destination for discerning travelers in Cortina d'Ampezzo.

Locanda Ai Santi Apostoli

Owner: Stefano Bianchi Michiel
Strada Nuova, 4391 / 30131 Venice / Italy
Telephone: ++390415212612 / Fax: ++390415212611
E-Mail: aisantia@tin.it / Web: www.veneziaweb.com/santiapostoli

★★★ **Price guide:** €182-€390 • Major credit cards accepted **Amenities:** • Air conditioning • Cable/satellite TV • Laundry • Airport: Venice • Nearby town: Venice • No restaurant • Breakfast included • Total rooms: 11; 2 canal, 1 superior, 1 standard & 1 family suite **Activities:** Boat rentals: water taxi & gondolas • Dock • Shopping • Tours or Merano: free **Additional Information:** They will book restaurants • Arrange tours

Roaming the streets of Venice, we came upon ancient doors with a regal brass plate specifying this was Locanda ai Santi Apostoli. Immediately drawn by the austere look, we rang the bell, entered through the courtyard, and traveled up the elevator. Stefano, the owner, was there to greet us. His warmth was comforting after spending the prior night on the third floor of a sweltering ghetto-like hotel, where the only source of cool air was a fan the night manager confiscated for his own benefit. The next morning after our breakfast of stale bread and weak cappuccino we departed. Fortunate we were to have arrived at this charming Locanda. Stefano was immediately sensitive to our situation, going out of his way to arrange congenial sleeping arrangements for our family, during a time when availability is not easy to come by.

If you have ever romanticized about living in a *palazzo* (palace) overlooking the Grand Canal of Venice, near the Ponte di Rialto, here's your opportunity. Both are visible from this 15th century Locanda on the third floor of this cherished ancestral home of Stefano. The Locanda is situated in a quiet residential area near Piazza San Marco, close to the Guggenheim Museum and the Academy, housing one of the finest art collections in Italy. The hotel has its own private dock, which is accessible for *gondolas* and motorboats. Breakfast was served in the living room overlooking the Grand Canal. The eleven guest rooms, although basic, are spacious with en-suite bathrooms and individual air conditioners, which we greatly appreciated. As you would expect, the two rooms opening onto the canal have the greatest appeal and demand. Additional beds can often be set up in the rooms to accommodate your kids. The staff is welcoming and responsive to the needs of families.

Miramonti Majestic Grand Hotel

Manager: Maurice Pratto
Peziè103 / 32043 Cortina d'Ampezzo (Bl) / Italy
Telephone: ++3904364201 / Fax: ++390436867019
E-Mail: hmirmonti.cortina@dolomiti.org / Web: www.cortina.dolomiti.org/hmiramonti

★★★★★ **Price Guide:** €103.29-€537.12 per person/per day • Major credit cards accepted **Amenities:** Air conditioning • Bar • Cable/Satellite TV • Internet • Laundry • Airports: Venice & Bolzano • Nearby towns: Belluno, and Cortina d' Ampezzo • Restaurant: Breakfast included; lunch & dinner à la carte • Total rooms: 105, plus 3 suites with jacuzzi **Activities:** Biking • Boat rentals which include rafting, canoeing, and sailing • Children's park • Fishing: Summer in nearby lakes of Ghedina, Pianozes, Scin and Boite River. • Golf: 9 holes • Gym • Hiking • Horseback riding • Massage • Sauna • Shopping: jewelry, antiques, high fashion, wine shops, and carpets • Skiing: nearby • Swimming pool: indoor • Tennis court • Cultural tours **Additional Information:** Cinema • Snooker table • Putting green • Rafting • Sailing • Jeep excursions • Bowling • All winter sports • Half board/full board

The Miramonti Majestic Grand Hotel is as captivating as the Dolomite Mountains that surround it. It's a resort for all seasons. Year-round, your family can make use of the indoor swimming pool, Jacuzzi, snooker table, wellness center (featuring massage, facials, cellulite treatment, sauna), and *Ambra Antica* (the exclusive ancient method of mud bath). In the summer, a playground for the children, tennis, golf, horseback riding, mountain bike, hiking, jeep excursions, canoeing, kayaking, rafting, and sailing are all obtainable. Cortina d'Ampezzo is one of the top winter sports resorts in the world. The mountain has the capacity to handle 40,000 skiers and snow boarders an hour with 150 kilometers of downhill runs appropriate for all levels

of ability. Impassioned cross-country skiers will enjoy 140 kilometers of trails plus off-mountain itineraries, along with nearby ice skating, snow rafting, and snow-mobiling. Consider taking your kids on a horse-drawn sleigh excursion.

Miramonti connects you to the town with its private shuttle service that departs every 30 minutes, a wonderful convenience for older children to maintain some independence. Cortina is a small, safe haven with many fashionable boutiques, cafes, restaurants, artistic, and cultural events. This grand hotel has been putting forth the best of Venetia's tradition since 1902. It has hosted royalty from around the globe as well as artistic greats such as Bridgette Bardot, Humphrey Bogart, Ingrid Bergman, Clark Gable,

Marcello Mastroiani, and "007's" Roger Moore. You will still experience the same peace and comfort amongst impressive mountain views as these individuals, with the advent of tastefully renovated rooms and modern amenities.

The warmth and friendliness that Mr. Pratto and his staff generate gives rise to an atmosphere of social gatherings. In the evening, as their pianist entertains you in the lounge, it is not unusual for the guests to join in dancing and singing. During our stay, there were numerous Jewish families from Rome. We all delighted in joining together for our traditional Horah dance to Hava Nagila and rounds of festive music. It was astounding for our children to recognize the commonality we shared with these distant kindred spirits. Next to the lounge is the Caminetto Bar. Besides their prime selection of local *grappa's* and pleasing cocktails, your kids will love tasting the eighteen different types of hot chocolate.

Mealtime, as in most of Italy, is an occasion to celebrate. Miramonti's palatial dining room, and the sheer quantity of food, evoked memories of the Catskill Mountains in upstate New York. The restaurant offers a vast selection of national and regional specialties. Be warned! An extensive fresh buffet only appears to be the entire dinner. Eat cautiously to save room for the other four courses. The kids enjoyed the vast array of food choices, with always something for everyone's particular taste. Venture with confidence to Miramonti Majestic Grand Hotel. They have covered all the bases including 24-hour concierge and medical assistance to ensure that you and your family have the vacation of your dreams.

Villa Franceschi Secolo XVI

Owner/Manager: Dal Corso Family
Via Don Minzoni, 28 / Mira Porte – Venezia / Italy
Telephone: ++39 041 4266531 / Fax: ++39 041 5608996
E-Mail: villafranceschi@tin.it / Web: www.villafranceschi.com

★★★★ **Price Guide:** €165-€439 • Major Credit Cards accepted **Amenities:** Air conditioning • Babysitting • Bar • TV • Internet • Laundry • Nearby airport is Venice • Nearest town is Mira Porta and Venice. • Restaurant. • Total number of rooms - 32 **Activities:** Biking • Boat Rental • Golf, 10km • Shopping in Venice; specialty Merano glass, Terme Abano • Tours of the Veneto, to include cultural, historic • Water park, Padovaland **Additional Information:** 24-hour concierge service • Bed and Breakfast €18 • Half board €45 • Full board €55

As we travel through Italy as a family, we discover that our enthusiasm is about undiscovered sites, culinary experiences, and the new people we meet along the way. The opportunity to revisit the Dal Corso family of Villa Margherita, and now their latest acquisition, the exquisite Villa Franceschi, is a gratifying highlight of our journey.

The Dal Corso family has done it again! Villa Franceschi stands on the beautiful Brenta River retaining its genuine Venetian atmosphere of the late 16th century. The villas built on the mainland along the river gave families then, and holiday goers now, a retreatful countryside escape, while allowing quick access to the city of Venice. These houses also gave the families an opportunity to show off their status. The 18th century engraver, Coronelli, gave us an idea of what Villa Franceschi must have looked like in his print titled "Palazzo Francheschi at Mira." Not much has changed in the two hundred years since the image was first illustrated. Today, this grand hotel once again reflects the Dal Corso's extreme attention to detail, evident in their thorough restoration.

There are thirty-two hotel rooms divided into two separate buildings. The main villa, which was near-completion during our visit, has two "noble floors," each with a central corridor and four junior suites. The second floor permits access to an extraordinary mansard-roof. Original marble fireplaces, epoch beams, and rare Venetian terra cotta tiling add authentic charm and beauty. The "Barchessa" (boat house) is the ancient rustic part of the property where boats, tools, and farm carts were housed. The eldest son, Alessandro Dal Corso, told me that the restoration of this building required the utmost care to main-

tain the original atmosphere. Valerie Dal Corso's impeccable taste creates a harmonious blend of Venetian terra cotta and wood. She has a designer's eye for combining artisan furniture with fine Italian fabrics. The Dal Corsos are delighted that the Barchessa's second floor has four suites that are the ideal solution for families with four to five people.

Both the villa and Barchessa are surrounded by romantic 18th century gardens representing the architectural theories of Andrea Palladio who designed villas for the cohesive effect of the gardens, riverbank, and water. Villa Francheschi's luxurious restaurant was presently open just for breakfast; however, Villa Margherita is just a five minute ride away, making it accessible for both lunch and dinner.

The Dal Corso's attention to detail continued throughout our dining experience. Uncannily, they seemed to remember our individual preferences for food and wine as though we had dined there the night before when, in fact, a year had passed. Returning to Villa Margherita's restaurant was a confirmation of their extraordinary cuisine and flawless hospitality. The boys unanimously agree, "It's the best!"

Villa Margherita

Owner: Dal Corso Family
Via Nazionale, 416/417 / 30030 Mira Porte (VE) / Italy
Telephone: ++390414265800 / Fax: ++390414265838
E-Mail: hvillam@tin.it / Web: www.villa-margherita.com

★★★★ **Price Guide:** €199–€350 • Major credit cards accepted **Amenities:** • Air conditioning • Bar • Cable/Satellite TV • Internet • Laundry • Airport: Venice • Nearby towns: Mira, Padua, and Venice • Restaurant: Breakfast included; lunch & dinner à la carte; closed Wednesdays. • Total rooms: 19 **Activities:** Biking • Boat rentals: canals • Children's park • Golf: 10 km • Massage: by appointment • Cultural tours: ancient palladium villas **Additional Information:** Open all year

The Dal Corso's open their doors for families to come celebrate an extreme form of hospitality reminiscent of the 17th and 18th century Patricians of Venice. Their brochure states, "The Dal Corso family, Remigio and Valeria, with their sons Alessandro and Dario, run both the hotel and restaurant with typically enthusiastic Italian style, assisted by excellent staff." Our experience of their skillful management and operations went well beyond "typical."

Villa Margherita is a journey worth taking merely to observe the relationship between the two brothers. They run this 15th century noble villa with the synchronicity of two figure skaters competing for a gold medal. The personal atten-

tion is unique, for at least one of the Dal Corsos are always accessible, making certain your family is properly taken care of. A tour of their prestigious Restaurant Margherita's kitchen revealed their grandmother working behind the scene assuring the quality and tradition of their food. The chef and owner of the restaurant is Remigio Dal Corso. Here, as in the movie *Chocolate*, eating these lovingly prepared artistic delicacies is a passionate and romantic experience. Traditional Venetian recipes and only the freshest available fish are used to satiate the appetites of the most discerning palates. Although the menu is extensively filled with rich and fascinating dishes, they take pleasure in preparing *Pasta Pomodora* (pasta with tomato sauce) just the way Isaac and Ari wanted it. As the other dishes arrived, however, they were seduced by the fragrant and imaginative visual presentation. Instantaneously, the kids had pushed aside their ordinary fare for great sea-salad dressed with aged balsamic vinegar, spaghetti with *scampi* (lobsters), mixed grilled fish, and *Risotto* (rice) with *scampi* and seasonal vegetables. When we physically felt we couldn't eat anymore, Dario escorted our family to the kitchen where Jacob, Isaac, and Ari, with the aid of the pastry chef, put decorative finishing touches on our desserts, fired a crème brule, and tasted fresh made chocolate.

The rooms that await you have been fashioned by Valeria Del Corso. Her choice of royal colors and fabric arouses your senses, and each contains satellite television and mini-bar. Throughout the Villa, you will discover many frescoed walls, sitting rooms, a bar, and a terrace used for breakfast during the warmer months.

The location of Villa Margherita is perfect, positioned on a picturesque angle of the Riviera del Brenta, opposite the most beautiful palladium villas designed for aristocratic families of the Serenissima Republic. It is situated in the town of Mira Porte, only ten kilometers from Venice and 15 kilometers from Padua. Directly outside the villa gate is the public bus to Venice. It is simple, and you avoid the possibility of getting lost and paying the exuberant costs of parking as we did.

Venice is filled with numerous sights and spectacles. Children and adults alike are lured by the fascination of her canals, with the Grand Canal being the widest. It begins at the *Stazione* (Station) and winds into St. Mark's basin. The adventure of continually being on and around water is mesmerizing to children. There are four modes of water transportation available: *Vaporetti* (water bus), *Motoscafi* (water taxi), and *gondolas* (Venetian boat), best used for slow sight seeing excursions. For our kids, just being on the 117 islands of Venice, 150 canals and 400 bridges, boating, scootering, and go-pedding, is "cool" in itself; nevertheless, there is much more to explore. The Island of Murano is a favorite for children as they can see how glass is made. The Naval Museum contains models of Venetian ships and uniforms depicting history through the 19th and 20th Centuries. Whether stopping into a few of the nearly 200 churches or learning the story of Venetian Jews with a visit to the "Ghetto," at the end of the day, step back through the gates of Villa Margherite where your family can relax in the peaceful park setting.

Emilia-Romagna

• Bologna

60

86
72 Florence
68 76 90 66
       80 78 64
    70
88   98
   82

74

84

Ancona
•
Marche

Perugia
•
92
96 Umbria
168

L'Aquila
• Abruzzo   100

Lazio
116 104
112
102 114 108
110 • Rome
106   120

Central Italy

Florence's Ponte Vecchio Bridge and Arno River

Tuscan countryside near the town of Montipulciano

Albergo Pietrasanta Palazzo Barsanti-Bonetti

Via Garibaldi, 35 / 55045 Pietrasanta (Lucca) / Italy
Manager: Marisa Giuliano
Telephone: ++390584793727 / Fax: ++390584793728
E-Mail: info@albergopietrasanta.com / Web: www.albergopietrasanta.com

★★★★ **Price Guide:** €180-€600 • Major credit cards accepted **Amenities:** Air conditioning • Baby sitting • Bar • Cable/Satellite TV • Internet • Laundry • Airports: Pisa and Florence • Nearby town: Forte dei Marmi, Pisa, Lucca, Florence, Genova • Restaurant: Breakfast; served until 2:00pm, €20/per person • Total rooms 20: 3 suites, 8 junior suites **Activities:** Biking • Boat rentals • Children's park • Fishing • Golf: 5 km at Versilia Golf Club • Gym • Horseback riding • Hiking • Massage: on request • Beach with swimming pool: nearby • Shopping: craft, antiques, marble shops, and fashion boutiques for children also. • Tennis court • Tours of small tourist train (replica of steam engine) for transiting around town; Torre di Pisa; Lucca; Collodi Park; Cinque Terre; Portofino; Acquario di Genova. **Additional Information:** Private garage: €15 • Special rates with nearby restaurants • Theater • Turkish Bath • Open year round

Situated along the coast between the sea and the mountains is the historical center of the artistic town Pietrasanta and neighboring Forte dei Marmi. Pietrasanta is located in Tuscany, near the Ligurian region. It is a safe seaside town with no vehicles permitted throughout the medieval streets and piazzas. This area has lent its splendor to many artists and writers who became captivated and inspired by its magnificence.

Mrs. Marisa Giuliano has been the director since its complete renovation and opening in August 1997. She, along with her colleagues, has transformed this grand 17th century palazzo into a quaint hotel. Over a glass of wine and antipasti, she shared with me her sentiments for Albergo Pietrasanta. "Here is like home and we want our guests to feel comfortable. Our casual bar is open and available for you to have a drink anywhere and any moment in time." The staff is warm and hospitable availing themselves continually to your total comfort and pleasure.

Special treatment of all their guests is typified by their eagerness to provide service beyond what's expected. Commonly, the reception has looked after a baby via a room monitor while the parents experience *la cucina tradizionale della Toscana* (traditional food of Tuscany) across the street at L' Enoteca, a gastronomic experience well suited for

the sophisticated pallet. While David and I savored some of their regional cuisine such as *Zuppa d'orzo con seppioline e fiori di zucca* (barley soup with squid and zucchini flowers), *insalata di funghi porcini e grana* (salad of porcini mushrooms and parmesan

cheese), the kids ran off into the *piazza* (town square) for a lighter fare of pizza and *gelato*. There are about ten restaurants within a two-minute walk from the hotel, each with their own special Tuscan style. Most restaurants in Pietrasanta, as throughout Italy, are child-friendly, especially in the summer when most Italian children stay awake quite late. Near the beach at Marina di Pietrasanta, my kids have singled out Il Nicchio Pizzeria Focacceria as their top choice.

Breakfast is served between 7:30 a.m. and 2:00 p.m., in the tropical window encased verandah, facing botanical landscaped gardens with century-old palm trees. Hot fresh croissants, breads, cakes, fruit, yogurt and, also at *à la carte* price, eggs prepared anyway you desire as just an example of the morning fare.

It is no wonder why people repeatedly return to this comfortable atmosphere, indicative of a fine private home. You may reserve, for your personal use during your entire stay, a fully equipped, modern workout suite with a Turkish bath. It opens onto a terraced patio overlooking the gardens. After an exhilarating workout and shower, unwind in the lounge chairs while calling room service to do the rest. As most gym facilities shun children, having our own workout room made exercising as a family relaxing and enjoyable.

Alberto Pietrasanta boasts twenty luxurious rooms, three suites, and eight junior suites. Each is designed and decorated to value the character of this ancient four-hundred-year-old palazzo. Contemporary artwork enhances the well-preserved frescoed ceilings. Many types of room configurations are available to suit the needs of your family. Reception will work with you to arrange the best possible situation. We had two sizable rooms with separate bathrooms, connected by a privately enclosed foyer.

Pietrasanta's location makes it ideal for explorations through both Tuscany and Ligurie. Take a day trip to the chic villages of Santa Margerita or Portofino. Walk, boat, or take a train through the five coastal towns of the Cinque Terre. You can go to Collodi near Pistoia and visit Pinocchio's Theme Park. Walk the ancient fortifications of Lucca before journeying on to its neighbor, Pisa. Tour the quarries where Michelangelo acquired his marble in the Massa Carrara province.

A highlight for the boys was the Acquario di Genova, built for the Expo '92 as a celebration of the 5th century of Christopher Columbus' discovery of the New World. This is one of Europe's largest aquariums. While Jacob developed a deeper appreciation of the Mediterranean biomes and the joy of coming face-to-face with sand digger sharks, Isaac was amused by the friskiness of the penguins and playfulness of the bottlenose dolphins. Ari, on the other hand, nearly fell head-first into the tactile tank of Ray's.

For a more laid-back and relaxed pace, the hotel will arrange a shuttle or bicycles to ride down to the wide expansive beaches of Versilia and exclusive shops of Forte dei Marmi. They have special rates with the beach resorts, restaurants, theaters, golf, tennis, and stables.

✎ Maranello, Italia ✎

The quintessence of speed, determination, and perseverance is captured in one glance at a Ferrari. The passion that goes into the manufacturing of these pieces of rocket art has driven enthusiasts of racing and car collectors to the town of Maranello, Italy, the birth-place of voluminous Ferrari automobiles and the site of the Scuderia Italia Formula One test track. Also located in Maranello are a myriad of stores specializing in Ferrari memorabilia and one of the most celebrated car museums in the world.

After driving for three exceptionally uncomfortable hours, my family and I finally managed to catch sight of the first sign to Maranello indicating we had twenty-five kilometers until we reached our destination; however, we became disconcerted when we later saw another sign reading fifty kilometers remained. Eventually, after receiving multiple sets of directions, we arrived to Maranello. Being that I have one of the most materialistic minds this world has ever known, I was ecstatic to arrive in this much raved home to the most desired automobile in the world. After discussing the Ferrari much of the ride, I received a hail storm of irate comments when we arrived to Maranello. There was not a single Ferrari in sight!

Determined to find what I sought, I frenetically asked everybody in sight where the raved about secrets of this town could be found. Finally, I came across a wandering American couple decorated in Ferrari memorabilia, who directed me towards a small, family-owned, Ferrari souvenir shop. I then made my first Ferrari purchase: a large seven by four foot flag. An Italian couple then informed me of the location of Maranello Ferrari Museum, or "L'anfiteatro." Here, the legend of Ferrari is captured. With three floors and multiple exhibits, L'anfiteatro is home to over thirty-one Ferrari automobiles including nine antique models such as the 250 Testarossa and an original wooden model.

After going through the museum and the enthusiast shops, I was still not satisfied because I was yet to see a Ferrari in action. As we began to drive away from the town, I heard a familiar zooming sound. When stepping out of the door of our car, I was taken aback by Ferrari music. It turns out that the day we had arrived, the 2002 Formula One car was being tested outside the factory on their track. They would drive a few laps every fifteen minutes and then go refuel. The intensity of the sound produced by the 2,997 cm^3 V10 Ferrari 3000 engine is enough to knock a heavy-weight to the ground. Moreover, the tremendous speeds reached, and the snapping of necks in a desperate attempt to follow the Ferrari, avail the chiropractor to great opportunity at the side of the track.

The enthusiasm of Ferrari stays with me even after leaving this enchanted town; therefore, I cannot conclude my analysis of Maranello. Instead, I hope that I have left you with the desire to visit this city and ignite the Ferrari passion in your own life.

Jacob Levinson

Hotel Restaurant Portole

Managing Proprietors: Mirella and Franco Lunghi
Via Umbro Cortonese, 36-52044 / Cortona (Arezzo) Italy
Telephone: ++ 39 0575 691008 / Fax: ++ 39 0575 691035
E-mail: portole@technet.it / Website: www.portole.it

★★★ **Price Guide:** €54–€93 • Major credit cards accepted • Nearest airport: Florence, Pisa or Rome • Nearest town: Cortona 7 km **Amenities:** 20 rooms • bathroom/shower • satellite TV • restaurant with capacity for 300 • conference/meeting room capacity 70 • parking • private garden • Panoramic terrace • Wine cellar **Activities:** Country trail walks and hikes • Cultural excursions to nearby towns • Mountain bike rides • Tennis **Additional Information:** Half board/ Full board available

Just days before leaving the United States, we received e-mail from our dear friend Stefano, who we wrote about in the *Forward;* a colleague and friend of his owns a hotel with a restaurant, heard we would be in the area reviewing potential properties and hoped Stefano could arrange for us to visit. At that point we were completely scheduled, but looked forward to joining them for dinner. As the trip progressed we were able to reorganize our plans, in order to spend additional time with Stefano, Frederica, their family, plus a night at Portole.

Hotel Restaurant Portole, traditionally built of local Tuscan Limestone, is a basic three star hotel with five star hospitality. It's situated on the Tuscan mountainside in the midst of woodland and countryside. This is a special location with its panoramic views across the Val di Chiana to Lake Trasimeno and Mount Amiata, along with being just a short ride from the ancient Etruscan town of Cortona and no more than forty kilometers to Arezzo and Pienza. Here you are surrounded by a vastness of hiking trails which extend all the way down through Cortona to Lake Trasimeno and beyond.

We arrived at Hotel Portole mid-day allowing ourselves enough time to take the kids to the water park in Cortona, meet Stefano and Frederica at his parents house, in the early evening, to be followed by dinner at Portole. As we drove down to Cortona, on the side of the road was a young man who appeared to be flagging us down. We thought perhaps he was experiencing car trouble. As we turned around to offer our help, we noticed a large bird freely soaring high above the mountains and over the Tuscan valley. Immediately, it became apparent that the man was the handler of this predatory looking bird. Cautiously exiting our car, the five of us moved slowly towards this amazing spectacle.

With an encouraging gesture of his hand to come closer, we suddenly became part of the personal relationship between this man and his bird. He introduced himself as Paolo Fontani one of approximately, one hundred and fifty Falconers' in Italy who train peregrine falcons and has been doing so since age ten. In the following hour we spent with Paolo, he took pride in enlightening us about these regal birds and their heritage. We learned that it was the 13th century, Italian-born German emperor Frederick II, who brought this royal art to Italy. Additionally, he explained the wind's effect on the way they fly; this particular day was calmer than the falcons prefer, however on gusty days they can reach heights of 2500 feet, then plummet down at speeds of about 200 miles per hour. Paolo then guided us up an adjacent mountain while still maintaining a visual and whistle like contact with his falcon, resembling the flapping of wings. While we stood within arms distance of Paolo, he reached into his pocket and then placed a fresh chicken head in his hand, which was protected by a specialized leather glove. Simultaneously waving a red flag like cloth with the opposite hand, he made a commanding sound to his falcon to return to him. Without delay, the falcon dove straight down; landing on the ground beside him, then up onto his arm, at once, aggressively devouring his earned prey. Paolo immediately placed a leather hood over the top of the peregrine's head, covering his eyes; apparently that which they can see only bothers the falcons. Jacob had the opportunity to hold this powerful majestic bird, bestowing upon him with a once in a life-

time experience that he will by no means ever forget. To enjoy the art of *falconeria* of Paolo Fontani, you can log on to www.lecontesse.com or call his mobile number at: + + 39 3287337390. We did eventually spend a short, but fun-filled time at the water park, along with a pleasurable visit at Stefano's families' farmhouse before returning back to Hotel Portole with Stefano and Frederica for dinner.

For an authentic Tuscan home cooking experience, look no further. Truly, above all, you come to Hotel Restaurant Portole for owner-chef Mirella Lunghi's traditional gastronomy, plus Franco Lunghi's genuine welcome. Her meals are prepared with regionally selected ingredients, most of which have been newly picked from their adjacent garden. Franco maintains a very good wine cellar, stocking some of the best Tuscan and Italian Wines. Nonetheless, his personal label *Portole* was a delightful accompaniment to Mirella's food.

The sight was exquisite: a charmingly set banquet size table, situated on the panoramic mountain terrace, with a Tuscan sun setting as the backdrop. Franco joined us for our feast, which began with *bruschetta* served with an array of delectable topping as our *antipasti*, and then bountiful plates of food continued for hours: grilled meats, potatoes, vegetables, salads and dessert. Isaac's enthusiasm over the meal drew

him into the kitchen to help Mirella slice and prepare the filets of Tuscan beef. As in all great Tuscan meals, you always end with traditional biscotti's immersed in a good strong *grappa*, for the perfect assimilation of the food and close to a flawless day and evening.

Castello Di Gargonza

Owner: Count Guicciardini Corsi Salviati
Loc. Gargonza / 52048 Monte San Savino, Arezzo / Italy
Telephone: ++390575847021 / Fax: ++390575847054
Restorante La Torre di Gargonza
Telephone: ++390575847065 / E-Mail: gargonza@gargonza.it
Web: www.gargonza.it

★★★ **Price guide:** €672–€1715 weekly/self-catering **Amenities:** Airports: Florence, Rome • Nearby towns: Arezzo, Cortona, Montepulciano, Monte San Savino, Perugia and Lake Trasimeno • Restaurant: includes breakfast; lunch & dinner à la carte • Total apartments: 23; 7 with TV & computer modems, 11 double bedrooms **Activities:** Hiking • Horseback riding • Swimming pool • Terme`: Rapolano • Cultural tours • Water park: Acqua Crocodile **Additional Information:** Meeting facilities • Cooking facilities • Additional bed: €48–€51

Castello di Gargonza is an incomparable experience to any property we have visited. Situated in the core of Tuscany's hills between Siena and Arezzo, it is a 13th century, fortified, medieval village, which has been transformed into guesthouses and apartments available for short and long-term rentals. Behind the ancient Sienese gates of this walled city lay its own church, store, swimming pool, restaurant, tower, gardens, and meeting rooms. Breakfast is served in the dining room, which houses the *Frantoio* (old olive press). The ancient private garden is a meditative place to sit, read, or savor a glass of Tuscano wine.

Many significant historical names are linked with Gargonza. In 1302, Dante Alighieri stayed here as a guest of the Ubertini family, owners of the property from 1285 to 1381. It was then passed on to the Republic of Siena who gave up Gargonza to the Seigniory of Florence; lastly, ownership was in the hands of Marchesi Corsi, descendants of Count Roberto Guicciardini, the present owner. He spent ten years restoring Gargonza and was sensitive to its initial standards and his ancestral roots. The Count watches over his village with the protectiveness of a father looking after his child. Count Guicciardini is a delightful, caring man with just enough eccentricity to have conceived this innovative concept for a hotel. He has five grown children of his own to whom he could pass on the responsibility of running the village; nevertheless, he is challenged by the prospect of someone else parenting his progeny.

This village resort provides you and your children the chance to be immersed in history and life, as it must have been centuries ago. The village resounds with the carefree existence of the former householders. Many of the domiciles maintain the original family names on the portals. There is "Pietrino," Pietro Rossi, a landowner and cultivator on the hill, who once owned this house. The "Niccolina" was the home of Niccolina Papini, who worked together with her mother Armida as a seamstress.

Restorante La Torre di Gargonza serves a wide variety of authentic Tuscan specialties in a comfortable family setting. Having your private kitchen offers you the choice to prepare simple meals. Most unforgettable was the afternoon we dined al fresco overlooking the extensive Val di Chiana below with salads of tomato, bufalo mozzarella, fresh greens, local olive oil and balsamic vinegar, cheeses, a loaf of Tuscan bread, and a bottle of wine.

We spent the remainder of the day in Rapolano Terme at Terme L'Antica Querciolara whose waters aid in the treatment and prevention of many respiratory disorders and related ailments, beneficial to both adults and children. Many spa treatments are available by the day or the week. The mineral-rich waters will leave your skin and joints enhanced and your soul invigorated. If you want to pick up the pace, visit the Aqua Park Crocodile (water park), go horseback-riding English style, or visit the surrounding legendary medieval villages of Arezzo, Siena, Monte San Savino, Perugia, Montepulciano, Cortona, and Lake Trasimeno.

Monte San Savino is the closest town to Gargonza, only 11 kilometers away. It is an ancient village where many indications of Etruscan civilizations have been discovered. Jews were present here at two separate times: first from 1421 to 1571 as pawn brokers, then 1627 to 1799 initially as pawnbrokers, then as a community. Monte San Savino still flourishes with local handicrafts and treasured pieces of pottery, dating back to the Renaissance and the Della Robbia School.

When we are traveling for several weeks at a time laundry piles up. In Monte San Savino we drove up to the *Lavanderia*, the car jam-packed with bags of dirty clothes. The owner of the business was wearing a cervical collar due to a recent injury from a motorcycle accident. David set up a makeshift chiropractic office, complete with the x-rays taken shortly after the crash. Following a brief examination and radiological analysis, David gave him a spinal adjustment. In appreciation, he washed, dried, folded, and perfectly packaged all of our clothes. This allowed us additional time for the guys to get their annual summer *Italiano* haircut. These artisans meticulously shear and arrange every strand of hair using both scissors and razor blades. Plan on one hour per cut, and be forewarned: they perform one style—short!

Castello di Gargonza's twenty-five houses are nestled within thick, luxurious woods. Numerous types of accommodations are available. There are apartments that provide lodging for two to ten people, or guest houses with seven double rooms, all equipped with private baths, shower, living room, telephone, kitchen area, or mini-bar. Most of the residences have been fully renovated fusing the Middle Ages with the 21st century. Gargonza is a rare extraordinary place. Here you can find serenity and inspiration while experiencing the best of Tuscany with your kids.

Castello Di Magona

Residenza d' Epoca / Owner: Dr. Cesare Merciai
Via di Venturina, 27 / I-57021 Campiglia Marittima, Livorno / Italy
Telephone: ++39 0565851235 / Fax: ++39 0565855127
E-Mail: relais@castellodimagona.it / Web: www.castellodimagona.it

★★★★ **Price guide:** €227.24–€624.91 • Major credit cards accepted **Amenities:** Air conditioning • Bar • Cable/Satellite TV • Internet • Airports: Florence, Pisa • Nearby towns: Bolgheri, Castagneto Carducci, Populonia, Massa Marittima, Volterra, Lucca, Pisa, Siena, Florence, Island of Elba. • Restaurant: Breakfast included; lunch & dinner à la carte • Total rooms: 11; 6 suites **Activities:** • Boat rental nearby • Golf • Gym • Hiking • Horseback riding: nearby • Massage: on request • Shopping • Swimming pool • Tennis court: nearby • Terme`: Calidario • Cultural tours • Water park: Acqua il Parco **Additional Information:** • Culinary classes • Painting lessons • Private chauffeured cars • Water park: Cavallino Matto amusement park • Half board/full board

This castle is one of the most important buildings in the Cornia valley. Dr. Cesare Merciai's family purchased Castello di Magona in 1860, and it is here that he spent his childhood and raised his own children. The castle dates back to the 1500's and has been the domicile of many Grand Dukes of Tuscany. This five bedroom, six-suite epoch residence perfectly combines the past and present to create magical moments. Upon entering the castle gates, you will be warmly welcomed by one of Dr. Merciai's gracious staff committed to making their home yours. They will organize special programs adapted to your family's particular interests.

Their capabilities are vast, whether you prefer private chauffeured excursions to Pisa or Lucca, tickets for the *Palio* (Siena's famous horse race), wine cellar tours with tastings at Sassicaia and Ornellaia, tickets for musical concerts of the region, special dinners, cooking classes, or horse-back riding. Close to Castello di Magona is Cavallino Matto amusement park, which opens at Easter and *Acqua il Parco* (water park). Perhaps if just the two of you would like to escape to the Island of Elba on a private boat, baby-sitting will be arranged. However, if your children have seafaring legs, in calm waters the boating is exceptional. We rented a 14-foot Boston Whaler and spent the day exploring the caves and beaches of Elba. The kids brought snorkels and we dove and swam off the boat. Pack a picnic lunch and plenty to drink. Content in a lounge chair or swimming in the pool, looking up at this majestic site was a surrealistic moment we will long remember. The boys and I took pleasure in spending a day at the castle exploring the elaborate garden grounds and complexities of this fortified residence. When David returned from golfing, our family was served a private lunch in the upper terraced garden.

Many fantastic artistic cities and natural riches surround Castello di Magona. There are major natural and archeological parks and nearby medieval villages such as Bolgheri, Castagneto Carducci, Volterra Suvereto, and Massa Marittima. Ideal for a special day of relaxation and tranquility, and set amongst Etruscan ruins, is the 36° Celsius thermal spring spa of Calidario, a complete holiday center with many available sports including tennis, horse-back riding, and trekking. As you unwind in the tranquility of the steamy healing waters, you can easily imagine the ancient people at play. The kids loved traversing through the small caves that led to a hydro-massage waterfall, swimming and diving off the board. As for us, just immersing ourselves in the therapeutic waters, or reclining poolside, was *perfecto*.

If you have ever dreamed of being Queen or King for a night, Castello Magona will suit your fantasies while meeting all your expectations, for it's an enchanting castle where dreams do come true.

Hotel Oasi Neumann

Owner/Manager: Umberto Geodone
Via delle Contesse, 1 / 52044 Cortona (AR) / Italy
Telephone: ++390575630354 / Fax: ++390575630477
E-Mail: info@hoteloasi.org / Web: www.hoteloasi.org

★★★ **Price guide:** €38.50-€100.00 per person • Major credit cards accepted **Amenities:** Bar • Cable/Satellite TVAirports: Florence, Rome • Nearby towns: Cortona, Montepulciano, Sansepolcro, Monterchi. • Restaurant: includes breakfast; lunch & dinner à la carte • Total rooms: 60 **Activities:** Biking • Park • Fishing • Golf • Hiking • Horseback riding • Shopping • Swimming pool: nearby • Tennis court: nearby • Cultural tours **Additional information:** Conference rooms • Additional beds: Discounts adults 15-20%, children ages 4-12 years 20-30% • Half board/full board

My family has the most endearing feelings for this once monastery, now hotel, located only seven hundred meters from Cortona's medieval village. As you may have read in our introduction, "Adjusting to Italy," here, on the Tuscan hillside, with a far-reaching view of the Val di Chiana and Lago Trasimeno area, is where our family's romance with Italy began.

Hotel Oasi was constructed at the end of the last century on the foundation of a 16th century medieval structure. Taking a step inside it will immediately foster an astute awareness of its mystical beginnings, a place that inspires artful thought and imagination. Artisans from far and wide travel here for her rousing spirit. Holiday travelers come for Hotel Oasi's tranquility, removed yet central to all Tuscany has to offer.

The interior is enchanting with its high cathedral ceilings and broad hallways. The simplicity of the furnishings complements the monastic atmosphere. Oasi's fifty bedrooms, many with sweeping panoramic views, are of considerable size. Their Tuscan Renaissance Restaurant serves traditional dishes rich in culture and authenticity. Breakfast is a plentiful buffet, whereas lunch and dinner offer table service. A barreled ceiling wine cellar avails itself for wine tasting. The courtyard with terraced gardens and fountain overlook the Tuscany valley below.

Although Hotel Oasi has no pool, they maintain a cooperative relationship with a nearby sports center, offering an array of activities including both tennis and swimming. One of the boys' favorite water parks, "Crocodile," is also in close proximity. Reception will assist in making reservations and arrangements for horseback riding, golf, and cooking classes. They can help you plan individual excursions to the accessible towns of Florence, Arezzo, Montepulciano, Siena, Perugia, Assisi, Gubbio, and Todi.

The town of Cortona was the birthplace of the Italian painter Luca Signorelli (1450-1523), a forerunner of Michelangelo. It is also the birthplace of Pietro da Cortona (1596-1669), an architect and painter of Roman baroque, as well as Gino Severini (1883-1966) who was part of the futurist movement. Cortona has two main piazzas: Piazza della Repubblica with its 13th century Palazzo Comunale and Piazza Signorelli, marked by the Palazzo Pretorio which houses the Museo dell'Accademia with its Etruscan museum displaying Egyptian, Roman, Medieval, and Renaissance pieces, and the Grand *Teatro* (theater). Cortona also has one of the best gelato shops in Italy, "Snoopy Ice Cream." After sampling through the regions, many others come close but never measure up in service, taste, price, and quantity. Jacob has said, "He appreciates that they are always willing to give many samples before you make your final choices."

The town contains several historic churches: the Church of the Gesu that now houses the Museo Diocesano, Santa Margherita, San Domenico, Santa Maria del Calcinaio, and San Niccolo. All are worth visiting. In the 14th century, Cortona was one of the Tuscan villages which permitted Jewish people to operate pawnshops and banks until they were required to move out to the ghettos of Siena and Florence in 1572. Today, there is no remaining evidence of Jewish life.

An exceptional restaurant is Trattoria Toscana on Via Vardano, run by a young couple, Max and Michelle. Coincidently, Max worked at the restaurant *Ciao Bella* in my hometown of Atlanta. His family has owned the restaurant for decades. Michelle is from New York and, while visiting Cortona, they fell in love, married, and have remained ever after.

The evenings in Cortona, as in most small medieval villages, are centered on family. Dinner usually begins around 9:00 p.m. and is often followed by a stroll in the *piazza* (town square), talking with friends and family, enjoying a *gelato* and the day's final *espresso*. In this type of environment, the kids feel safe and sound going off on their own joining a game of soccer or tag with the native Italian kids.

Hotel Oasi Neumann will accommodate your family any way they can. Be sure to ask about their family rooms. Bring a journal, sketchpad, and a palette, for you are sure to be inspired.

Hotel Regency

Owner: Sig. Amedeo Ottaviani
General Manager: Andrea L. Luri
Piazza Massimo d'Azeglio 3 / 50121 Florence, Italy
Tel: ++39 055245247 / Fax: ++39 0552346735
E-mail: info@regency-hotel.com / Website: www.hotel-regency.com

★★★★★ **Price Guide:** €270-€800 per room/per day • includes generous buffet breakfast • Major credit cards accepted • Nearest Airport: Florence's Amerigo Vespucci International Airport • Nearest Town: Florence **Amenities:** Located in the heart of Florence • 34 rooms and suites, including honeymoon suite in garden with private patio, all elegantly furnished • Fully air-conditioned • Satellite color television • In-room electronic safe • Room service • Multi-lingual staff • Garage with valet service • Limousine airport transfer and privately chauffeured excursions upon request • World renown gourmet restaurant *Relais Le Jardin:* serving breakfast, lunch, and dinner; exceptional wine list **Activities:** Sightseeing • Museums • Shopping • highlights for kid's: Science Museum, Specola Museum with reproductions of bodies dating back centuries, Accademia has special section dedicated to ancient musical instruments, a scanner for *The David* provides an inside view of the statue • Galileo observatory in Arceteri/20 minutes • Biking • Tennis nearby • Ugolino Golf Course 13 kilometers away **Additional Information:** Banquet facilities for up to 30 people • Extra bed available in Double Room Deluxe • Junior Suite and Suites

It's immediately apparent upon entering the *piazza* in which Hotel Regency is located that you have found just the perfect getaway. This is a peaceful oasis, in the middle of the artistic city of Florence. What's more, it's across from a large park with a carousel, plus lots of space for the kids to run and play. Flawless renovations have transformed this once private villa into a premier five star property. Mr. Ottaviani, who is both the proprietor of Hotel Regency as well as Hotel

Lord Byron, has an impeccable eye for detail and design. Everywhere you look in the sitting rooms, hallways, guestrooms, restaurant, and garden is a refined sense of beauty.

The ease in which we were able to stroll just minutes from the hotel to many of the important highlights of Florence was pleasurable. This enabled us to explore the city in stages, returning to Hotel Regency for a quick respite. After lunch in the private garden under the shade trees, we felt relaxed and refreshed to see the rest of the sights.

Each time we return to Italy, the kids are older and open to new experiences and tastes. This journey brought the discovery of *Tartufo* or Truffles, to Isaac. At one time Truffles were forms of exchange among the noble; nowadays they're readily available to all. He tasted them as *antipasti* on breads, in meats, vegetables and even as dessert in *gelato*. We explored many shops along the *strada's* of Florence in search of these valuable pieces of earthy flavor. He found *Boscovivo* located on Borgo Albizi 85/87R, one hundred meters from the *Duomo Santa Maria del Fiori.* This is an exclusive shop specializing in truffles of every imaginable form such as, Fresh Truffles, Truffles in Brine, Truffle *Carpaccio*, Truffle Cheese, Truffle Creams & Flavored Oils, and an array of typical Tuscan specialty items. After conferring with the store's proprietor about the proper preparation, he bought a sealed jar of whole *Tartufo*, specifically the summer black truffle known as *Scorzone* or *Tuber Aestivum Vitt.,* along with the proper grating utensil. You can visit online at www.boscovivo.it or call + +39 0552001447.

In the late afternoons, we retreated to our richly furnished suite of rooms at the Regency, allowing ourselves enough time to prepare for dinner in a relaxed manner: a luxurious bath enhanced by their special *Vintage* products, and wine in the hotel's intimate garden. Dinner at the Regency's restaurant *Relais le Jardin* is an event that will linger on, long after the pleasures of eating. The dining rooms are chic yet uphold the allure of its regal Florentine past. The cuisine is both original and artistic while generating the true passions of authentic Tuscan flavors. The table service is above reproach, bringing into being a perfect dining experience. One evening Ari couldn't decide between *Gnocchi* and a Tuscan Filet, thus they brought both. Jacob just couldn't get enough of their *antipasti* of freshly smoked, thinly sliced swordfish, which he had them prepare entrée size. Certainly, our boys didn't develop these sophisticated tastes overnight. With time and continual exposure, kids can learn anything.

The kind staff's warm welcome and genuine desire to help, further enhance the meticulous attributes of this fine villa, leaving your family with few, if any, additional requirements.

Hotel Villa Clodia

Owner: Giancarlo Ghezzi / Managers: Stefano and Deborach Bonanni
Via Italia 43 / 58050 Saturnia (GR) / Italy
Telephone: ++390564601212 / Fax: ++390564601305
E-mail: villaclodia@laltrameremma.it / Web: www.saturniaonline.it

★★★ **Price guide:** €88-€100 per person • Major credit cards accepted **Amenities:** Air conditioning • Cable/Satellite TV • Airport: Rome • Nearby towns: Saturnia, Manciano, Montemerano, Poggio Murella, Pitigliano, Semproniano, Sovana, Grosseto, Massa, Marittima and Voltera • Restaurant: none • Breakfast included • Total rooms: 10, including 2 suites **Activities:** • Swimming pool • Terme`: Saturnia **Additional Information:** • Closed in December

Since 1998, we have sojourned yearly to visit Stefano and Deborach at Hotel Villa Clodia. The grandness of this slight villa lies in the genuineness of this couple. The owner, Giancarlo Ghezzi, is Stefano's uncle, but he and Deborach have managed and supervised the hotel since 1997. Stefano's talents go well beyond his administrative ability. He is accomplished on both keyboard and accordion. Upon request in advance, he and his singing accompanist, Sonia, will perform poolside for your family. Deborach's perpetual smile and thoughtful ways promise a comfortable stay.

Villa Clodia is magnificently perched at the brim of this quaint village crested over the undulating hills of Tuscany. As you peer below, the Terme di Saturnia comes into view. This Terme, where the water cascades out at a velocity of eight hundred liters (which is 160 gallons) per second with a continual temperature of 37° celsius (98.6 fahrenheit) constructing little pools in a natural crater is, along with the Cinque Terre, our kids' favorite spot.

Sacred powers and therapeutic assets of the "Baths of Saturnia" date back to pre-Roman age. These healing waters have been fought over by the Aldobrandeschi family from Santa Fiora and the Aldobrandeschi from Sovana. Nevertheless, even though the town of Saturnia was allocated to Sovana County, the thermal waters were not part of the separation and would continue on as a mutual ownership between the states. People were still entitled to take pleasure in this inherent volcanic spring regardless of the boundaries that subdivided them. *The Guide to the Thermal Treatments*, published by world-renowned spa and first class resort at Terme di Saturnia, concludes, "The sulfurous waters of Saturnia represent a perfect physiological treatment in all cases and at any age."

Each year we return to what we consider "our room," the family suite with its private balcony and panoramic view. Villa Clodia has ten rooms and two suites. All the rooms are pleasantly furnished with a mini-bar, TV, and private bathrooms. The

pool is nestled within the garden permitting views of the picturesque valley below.

One date remains vivid for us when Isaac was not feeling well on July 14, 2001. It was his twelfth birthday, so to aid in his recovery, Deborach continually replenished trays of tea, honey, and biscotti. Her attentiveness was that of a caring aunt. If you are lucky, she will teach you the secret of the "cappuccino flower!" The sad, but humorous, part of Isaac's birthday is that when "Ristorante Melangolo" overheard that it was his special day, they secretly baked a grandiose cake, but Isaac was fast asleep by the time we lit the candles that evening. We were leaving Villa Clodia the next morning and the cake could not travel well; therefore, we all sang happy birthday that evening and ate the cake in his honor. It wasn't until two days had past that we officially ushered in his twelfth birthday at "La Posta Vecchia (central Italy)."

Hotel Villa Villoresi

Owner: Cristina Villoresi
loc. Colonnata / Via Ciampi, 2 / 50019 Sesto Fiorentino, Florence / Italy
Telephone: ++39055443212 / Fax: ++39055442063
E-Mail: cvillor@tin.it / Web: www.ila-chateau.com/villoresi/

★★★ **Price Guide:** €160–€260 **Amenities:** Bar • Airport: Florence • Nearby towns: Florence, Siena and Bologna • Restaurant: Breakfast included; lunch & dinner à la carte • Total rooms: 28, 5 suites. **Activities:** • Children's park • Shopping: leather • Swimming pool • Cultural tours **Additional Information:** • Culinary classes • Programs: Renaissance in Tuscany, or other cities and time periods • Perfumery: create your personal scent • Open all year • Half board/full board

Located just five miles from the center of Florence is the Hotel Villa Villoresi, a registered national monument. Built as a fortress in the 12th century, the villa is a splendid representation of Renaissance architecture and art. One of the earliest representations of the *retour d' Egypte* (return to Egypt) existing in Italy resides here at the Villa as a 40-meter long entrance gallery that was originally a passage for horses. In 1928, it was entirely painted by A. Luzzi with Tuscan landscapes and Egyptian symbols. Villa Villoresi was converted into a hotel in the 1960s. This three star hotel boasts the longest terrace or renaissance *loggia* in Tuscany, which overlooks their Italian gardens and swimming pool. It encompasses some of the most attractive rooms of the villa containing frescoes and antiques while opening onto this *loggia*. We also recommend "the music room" which is large and spacious. Jacob commented that he, "…particularly enjoyed staying on the outskirts of Florence in that the city tends to be busy and noisy at night, making it difficult to sleep."

The hotel's manager, Countess Cristina Villoresi, represents eight centuries and five Villoresi actual property owners. We spent the afternoon in the villa's courtyard speaking with the Countess; her knowledge of art and history coupled with family legends is enchanting. One of the countless stories she told was of "Gemma Donati," Dante's wife, who stayed in this villa as a refugee for a period of time during the poet's exile. Countess Cristina is encouraging of family travel and believes that an eminent factor in enjoying yourselves in Italy is to "give up your preconceived ideas and be open to new possibilities."

Countess Cristina is always ready to host larger festive celebrations accompanied by music, gourmet dinners, cocktail parties, and receptions. Several programs designed for small groups of twelve to twenty people are available on diverse aspects of the Renaissance in Tuscany. The program's duration is from two through fourteen days. They can curtail their courses to suit your specific needs and interests. These classes are also available for university students in addition to precocious children.

Hotel Villa Villoresi's restaurant consists of two dining rooms which are located in the medieval part of the villa; one is located in the courtyard, the other situated in the park where we savored their simple, tasty Tuscan home cooking. During the summer months, light lunches are served poolside. Many of the dishes are Villoresi's own recipes accompanied by fresh herbs, fresh vegetables, and fruit from their own garden. They prefer to offer a limited menu of choice fresh foods. The local cheese and wines of the region are exquisite.

Lorenzo Villoresi, Cristina's brother, practices the art of perfumery in his studio overlooking the rooftops of Florence. It has been said that, "To enter his laboratory is to discover the world where the senses are one's only guide." His original collections of personal fragrances, perfumes, accessories for the bath and the home, have drawn worldwide acclaim. Private appointments to create your personal scent may be arranged through Villa Villoresi.

Il Borro

Luxury Apartment & Villa Rentals
Owner: Salvatore Ferragamo Family / Manager: Gloria Amico
52020 San Giustino Valdarno (Arezzo) / Italy
Telephone: ++39 055 977053 / Fax: ++39 055 977055
E-Mail: ilborro@ilborro.it / Web: www.ilborro.it

★★★★★ **Price Guide:** €697–€2,566 per week per apartment with 3-4 people, daily rates available • Credit Cards accepted, Visa, MasterCard **Amenities:** Baby sitting • Bar • TV • Internet • Laundry • Nearby airports are Florence, Rome or Pisa • Nearest town is Arezzo, Florence and Siena • Restaurant: Nearby village of Il Borro • Total number of rooms: 19 apartments **Activities:** Biking • Fishing • Driving range • Hiking • Horseback riding • Massage • Shopping at fashion designer outlets • Swimming pools • Cultural, historic, city, shopping, and winery tours **Additional Information:** Hot air ballooning, gliding lessons • Classes offered: watercolor painting, *tromp l'oeil*, cooking • Services: cook, car hire, information for places to go with children. Weddings, anniversaries, and other formal or informal events

～⌒～

In the beginning of the last century, the estate was bought by Amadeo, Duke of Aosta, and cousin of the heir to the throne of Italy. During World War II, the villa was destroyed by Germans. The Salvatore Ferragamo family has now restored the villa and estate to its past glory. Although Il Borro extends over 700 *hectares* (0.40 = 1 acre), its idyllic village with medieval architecture still is the core of activity.

Dispersed over the surrounding land are typical Tuscan farmhouses, which were originally the "master's houses." These beloved properties have been luxuriously restored to maintain their rustic origins and now offer first class comfort. Each of the villas vary with individual character and charm; however, all the houses and apartments have a fully modern kitchen with refrigerator-freezer, dishwasher, stove, oven, household china, utensils, and a washing machine. Deluxe bathrooms contain shower, bath, double faucet unit, toilet, bidet, mirrors, and fresh towels. The beds will be made up prior to your family's arrival with fresh linens suitable to the season. As you relax around the open fire of your villa, or lounge by the swimming pool, depending on the season, it will be apparent that the Ferragamos have considered every detail of each house.

"Poggio Piano" was the name of our home on the Borro estate. Just off a narrow unpaved road, which curves through fields of sunflowers on the property, was this grand colonial farmhouse. The home is divided into four apartments, two on each level. Our ground-floor residence, with separate entranceways accommodated our family with ease.

Immediately upon entering *La Cucina* (the kitchen) of our abode, we felt the personal touch of the Ferragamos. A basket filled with Il Borro produce welcomes all their guests. Furthermore, local artisans who are available to reproduce and ship any item virtually anywhere in the world make the furniture in the homes.

The swimming pool with stone barbecue serves as a social area to meet the other families on holiday. L'Osteria del Borro, a casual yet elegant restaurant, prepares traditional Tuscan foods made from locally grown Borro products. The food served family style was plentiful. L'Osteria is closed Wednesdays at which time the chef is available for personal hire. Inform him of your preferences, and he will create a menu accompanied by Tuscany's fine wines.

The Ferragamos have created a booklet containing all essential information. They include an operational manual listing the appliances, restaurants in the area, antique markets, the high fashion outlets of Prada, Dolce E Gabbana, Fendi, Armani, and Gucci, and museums in which they will book your tickets including their very own museum of over 10,000 Salvatore Ferragamo shoes in Florence. If you should desire site-seeing, shopping, or winery excursions through Tuscany or Umbria, inform the office three days in advance, and they will arrange the day trips for your family.

We found many activities to see and do around the estate such as: mountain biking, hiking, fishing, gliding lessons, and hot air ballooning. Picnics, horseback riding lessons and trail rides are also available. We confidently placed our kids with varying degree of equestrian experience in the hands of Alison Sanford, the riding instructor. Il Borro also offers the possibility of various weeklong courses in

watercolor painting, *tromp l'oeil*, and Tuscan cookery. The Il Borro estate is a tribute to the brilliance and foresight of this artistic family with their pivotal role in international fashion and luxury vacations. Salvadore Ferragamo was known as the "shoemaker of dreams." To us, Il Borro is the "holiday maker of dreams." A stay at the Ferragamo's estate is as divine as a walk in their designer shoes.

Il Pozzetto

Residence / Owner: Monique Kraft / Manager: Sandra & Giuseppe Michelognoli (Monique's Son)
Via Casale, 16 / 52031 Anghiari (Arezzo) / Italy
Telephone: ++390575723248 / Reservations: ++39055284273
Fax: ++390552398267 / E-Mail: g.michelognoli@tin.it / Web: www.ilpozzeto.it

★★★ **Price guide:** €54–€110 daily rate per person, €900–€1260 per week **Amenities:** Cable/Satellite TV • Laundry • Airport: Florence • Closest towns: Anghiari, Sansepolcro, Cortona, Arezzo, Perugia, Gubbio, Assisi, and Siena • Restaurant: none • Total apartments: 8 **Activities:** Biking • Hiking • Horseback riding: nearby **Additional Information:** Private parking • Jacuzzi suites • Movies: on premise • Piano bar • Meals available upon request

After traveling nomadically for two weeks without a reservation, we recognized that it was time to take up residence for a while. We found Il Pozzetto, situated between Arezzo, Cortona, and Sansepolcro. This former 17th century Franciscan Friar's monastery is located 7 kilometers from Anghiari. To reach this private villa, we followed an unpaved, winding road for 5 kilometers. The path seemed so remote that we turned back to Anghiari to confirm our direc-

tion. It was at this point we met Vicenzo Calli, an eminent painter, whose artistry is exhibited worldwide. The studio is below his family's antique shop where we stopped for directions. After several impressionable hours viewing the Calli family valuable pieces and Vicenzo's expressionistic compositions, he boarded his Duccatti motorcycle to lead the way to Il Pozzetto.

You would never imagine such an extraordinary place could exist at this altitude. Il Pozzetto is the ideal place for families who love to spend their holidays enveloped in nature. From the hill-top where Il Pozzetto sits, the view is breathtaking. It has been said that at Il Pozzetto, nature becomes the master and you almost forget that everyday life is right at the bottom. Staying here offered us the balance of enjoying the nearby Tuscan cities and retreating back to the rich nature that surrounds this hermitage.

The main villa is composed of several apartments that contain two to six beds, bath, or shower. The décor throughout is typical of Tuscan country life, integrated with modern amenities that include kitchenette, satellite TV, and heating. There is also a family community room with a fireplace, books, and games. We stayed in the farmhouse adjacent to the larger villa complete with two bedrooms, a large living room with two studio beds, dining room, kitchen, and bathroom, all opening onto a dining patio.

On arrival to our quarters, Ari had to use the toilette. Unaccustomed to the antiquity of this ancient home, he removed the key from the outside of the door before entering, promptly locking himself in. The only way out was to either remove the door, or to have him throw the key through a hole in the wall four to five inches in diameter, five feet above his head, leading to the exterior of the villa. The caretaker of Il Pozzetto, David, his brothers, and I coaxed and cheered him on for an extended amount of time. All of a sudden, the key shot out the miniscule orifice, and he was free at last.

The most magnificent sweeping vistas of hills and fields of sunflowers can be appreciated from the terrace of the swimming pool. To further enhance your family's enjoyment together, an outdoor kitchen with a brick-oven awaits you pool side. We would go into town each afternoon to pick out fresh produce, pasta, breads, and desserts for dinner. The boys took great pleasure in picking the wild lavender, basil, sage, and rosemary encircling our stone villa. Isaac would then prepare a salad dressing of olive oil with balsamic vinegar infused with these herbs. I cooked simple sauces to accompany the freshly made pasta. We befriended a Danish family visiting with their two boys who joined us for meals as well.

I sat each evening outside on the terrace surrounded by the still nights, cowbells in the distance, and serenading crickets. As I chronicled my thoughts, ideas began to formulate as to how I could encourage other families to spend more quality time together, simply enjoying life. The dream of *Italy's Best with Kids* was conceived.

Montorio Country Residence

Owner/Manager: Stefania Savini
Strada per Pienza, 2 / 53045 Montepulciano (Siena), Italy
Tel: ++39 0578 717442 / Fax: ++39 0578 715456
E-mail: info@montorio.com / Website: www.montorio.com

★★★★ **Price Guide:** From €750–€1200 per week per 2 person and €1700 per 4 person • meals not included • Credit cards accepted: Visa, MasterCard • Laundry • Nearest airport: Florence's Amerigo Vespucci International 100 km, Rome's Fiumicino 150km • Nearest town: Montepulciano, Arezzo 50km, Siena 60km, Perugia 60km **Amenities:** 5 apartments: 3/1 bedroom, 2/2 bedrooms • Entire residence can be reserved • Private bathrooms • Kitchens • fireplaces • Telephones with direct external line • Satellite television • Parking • Cleaning service daily excluding Sunday's and Italian national holidays • Laundry **Activities:** The owner, Stefania Savini invites your family to get in touch with her in regard to information on local tours and excursions • shopping • wine tours • cultural tours • numerous hot water *terme's* or spa's to take a dip in all over the surrounding area **Additional Information:** Remote security gate to be installed for 2004/2005 season • Closing period: December 15th to January 15th • Children 15 years and up are welcomed • animals are not allowed • contact in advance by e-mail to have food stocked in refrigerator or specific provisions available upon arrival

Montorio is to be found majestically positioned 600 meters above sea level with a view that looks out over a scene of exceptional beauty. This historic country Residence offers a 360 degree panoramic view which encompasses the Temple of San Biagio, one of the most important monuments of the Italian Renaissance, designed by Antonio Sangallo il Vecchio; cypresses, olive trees, and vineyards; the enchanting town of Montepulciano with its important works of art from the Renaissance period, and unique underground caves, world renowned wines, cheeses, and Tuscan specialty shops.

The interior of Montorio's five apartments is a simple but tasteful Tuscan décor with terracotta floors, wrought iron lights produced by Florentine craftsmanship, antique furniture, paintings, and complete with up-to-the-minute amenities. The private separate dwellings all within a single compound make this is a wonderful holiday retreat for an extended family to rent in its entirety.

Although there is no pool, a short distance from Montorio are several thermal spas. We have visited most of them, but I can say with almost total assurance that *Bagni San Filippo*, in the province of Siena, is one of the most inspirational. These spas are known for curing respiratory tract, ear, nose, and throat problems; arthritic and rheumatic diseases; skin diseases; regain bodily shape; and stress management. There are two options here, which enable you to take pleasure in these special healing waters; for a more civilized experience, you can pay an admission fee to use the lovely Bagni San Filippo pool that has a steaming waterfall and natural whirlpool, wellness facility, snack bar, plus bathrooms with showers. This is where many eminent Romans, such as Lorenzo il Magnifico and the sanctified Florentine Filippo Benzi, came for extended periods of time to rejuvenate their spirit. However, we prefer the little stream called *Fossa Bianco* that runs wild, forming natural warm sulfuric pools as it bends and caresses the calcareous rocks along the way. The approach is simple: you must enter through a dirt road just outside San Filippo, and follow the path as it winds through the trees to the totally white water pools with a soft clay bottom. Either choice will rejuvenate your body, mind, and soul giving you a deep sense of relaxation. Complete the experience with a peaceful meal in the quaint little town before heading back to Montorio. Contact Terme San Filippo at www.termesanfilippo.it or call ++39 0577 872982 for additional information.

Herbs of rosemary and lavender, terracotta pots and flowers, alongside ancient trees, surround the grounds of the residence. Lounge chairs and modern picnic tables with umbrellas are strategically positioned throughout the hilltop, always offering outstanding vista along with an ideal spot for reading, drinking a glass of Montepulciano's *Vino Nobile* red wine, and family dinners. In fact, one particular evening, Isaac was having a hankering to cook us a steak dinner; he insisted that we drive him to the local *Coop* or grocery store for the necessary food supplies. The displays of breads, cheeses, pastas, vegetables, and fruits are so alluring; repeatedly we buy more than we can eat, as we did on this particular shopping excursion. The *Coop* is an excellent place to purchase inexpensive fine wines, coffee beans, select olive oils, and balsamic vinegars. With limited pans, utensils, and ingredients, Isaac marinated and sautéed the beef in olive oil, aged bal-

samic vinegar, and freshly picked rosemary from the property. Lastly, he roasted tomatoes in a saucepan, than gracefully covered the prepared dish. Collectively, we set the table with all our provisions in the little *piazza* outside our apartment and enjoyed an unforgettable evening under the stars accompanied by a cool gentle Tuscan breeze.

Bocce, the typical past-time game of Italian men throughout Italy, is played close by in the park just outside the gates of Montepulciano. For a classic look at this age-old game, show up any Friday or Saturday night around sunset. No need to rush since the games go through mid-night. Surrounding the playing field are Italian families eating gelato, sipping espresso, kids riding the carrousel, while at the same time cheering on their favorite players. This particular park is one of the nicest we've seen, with well manicured courts and finely dressed distinguished gentleman competing for both fun and fortune. The kids were so enthralled and fascinated by the game that they videoed and photographed the unique mannerisms of the players. The men appeared to enjoy the attention along with the sincere interest of our kids in their game and affectionately referred to them as the "*the paparazzi.*"

Montorio is an idyllic place for those who value a peaceful heaven to enjoy the serene views while pondering life. Stefania stated it well when she said, "Here you will find what you expected from Tuscany, beyond what the *Euro* can buy: eye-catching art combined with nature."

San Biagio Relais

Owner: Gianfranco Magnosi Family
Via Dante, 34 / 58015 Orbetello (Grosseto) / Italy
Telephone: ++390564860543 or 85008 / Fax: ++390564867787
E-Mail: sanbiagiorealis@sanbiagiorealis.com / Web: www.sanbiagiorelais.com

★★★★ **Price guide:** €120–€240, Extra bed €35 • Major credit cards accepted **Amenities:** Air conditioning • Bar • Cable/Satellite TV • Airports: Florence, Rome • Nearby towns: Orbetello, Giglio Island, Porto Ercole, Porto Santo Stefano, Grosetto • Restaurant: none • Meals included: Breakfast • Total rooms: 13; suites: 4 **Activities:** • Biking • Boat rentals • Golf: Maremmello Golf Club • Horseback riding • Beach: nearby • Shopping • Terme`: Saturnia • Excursions arranged: Visits to the Oasis of Orbetello, Talamone, and Uccellina Park, Lake Burano natural reserve, drive the castle roads

We fell in love with this alluring seaside town of Orbetello. After many excursions to its neighboring islands and villages, Orbetello has a quiet sophistication making it a more desirable destination. The town emerges at the pinnacle of a small island, which is surrounded by two lagoons, Levante and Ponente. Two strips of sandbars offering miles of wonderful beaches separate these lagoons.

Tired and exhausted from a disappointing journey to Giglio Island, we ventured into the tourist information office of Orbetello. Helpful and efficient, they gave us a few available suggestions. However, upon walking through the impressive arched entranceway we were warmly greeted by Sonia, the manager who, assured us this noble *palazzo* (palace) was home for the night.

San Biagio Relais is an exquisite ancient residence, which maintains an aura of elegance and charm. The thirteen rooms and four suites each have their own distinctive décor. The painted frescos and antiques that adorn each room add a unique artistic character. The suites are spacious as is the shared parlor that joins them, providing our family ample room.

San Biagio's attractive and cozy verandah with a bar serves a nice breakfast. Ari, so comfortable in this discreet home, wandered down to join us for our morning

meal in his sleeping attire. Although they do not have a restaurant, Orbetello boasts many first rate Etruscan choices a few steps from the hotel. This is a perfect location to explore the surrounding territory. The hotel staff is happy to assist your family in developing an itinerary, Maremmello Golf Club, horseback riding, bike, and boat rentals can also be arranged.

Villa Gamberaia-Zalum

Owner: Dott. (Dr.) Luigi Zalum
Via del Rossellino, 72-50135 / Settignano (Florence), Italy
Tel: ++39 055 697205 / Fax: ++39 055 697090
E-mail: villagam@tin.it / Website: www.villagamberaia.com

★★★★ **Price Guide:** €250-€400/per day/breakfast included • €2,200-€4,400/per week • €18, 000/per week/6 rooms, 5 bathrooms, living room, dinning room, kitchen, plus three personnel • all weekly rates include breakfast, daily cleaning, sheet change two times • Major credit cards accepted • Nearest airport: Florence's Amerigo Vespucci International • Nearest town: Florence 6 km, Settignano, 800 meters **Amenities:** 10 rooms • Parking • Air conditioning/ Heating • laundry • Mini-bar • Color and satellite TV • 17th century Italian gardens • swimming pool • two elegantly appointed salons • interior colonnade courtyard, and various administrative or meeting spaces available for receptions, conferences, exhibits, and other functions with 250 seats **Activities:** Bicycle rentals 2 km • Golf 15 km • Horse riding 2 km • Tennis 3km • Shopping • Wine tours • Cultural tours • Garden tours of Villa Gamberaia-Zalum **Additional Information:** By request in advance of your stay, you may hire a chef • Open all year • Pets are not allowed

Upon entering the gates of Villa Gamberaia with its guarding cypresses leading our way up towards the main villa, I was overcome by a silent grandeur; my eyes beheld the most brilliant views of Florence and the contiguous Arno valley, with superb gardens fêted throughout the world by salient landscape architects and garden historians.

Villa Gamberaia's history is extensive, beginning in the 14th century as a farmhouse belonging to the Convent of S. Martino a Mensola, and through to the 18th century when the Florentine noble Zanobi Lapi, who laid out the gardens,

owned it and passed into the hands of the Marchesi Capponi. In 1896, Princess Giovanna Ghika, sister of Queen Natalie of Serbia, obtained Villa Gamberaia and the restoration of the gardens was begun by transforming the *parterre de broderie* into the *parterre d'eau*. The next owner was American-born Mithilda Ledyard Cass, Baroness von Ketteler. In 1954, after the Villa was partially destroyed during WWII, Marcello Marchi and his wife Nerina von Erdberg acquired the Gamberaia, making careful, but extensive renovations to the villa and gardens. In 1994, he passed the villa on to his daughter Franca and her husband Luigi Zalum who continue the ongoing work of preservation and restoration.

Dr. Zalum is a refined man who, quietly and without airs, takes pleasure in the regal splendor of his notable domain. He invited us up to his home one evening above Villa Gamberaia, ingratiating us with his presence while his attentive staff served drinks and dessert. Ari and Isaac swam in his pool while David, Jacob, and I enjoyed poignant conversation with the doctor. He took a special interest in Jacob, quizzical about his interests and life experiences. Jacob in turn respected the sage advice of this most distinguished gentleman.

Dr. Zalum is particular about who visits his extraordinary Villa Gamberaia. Everyone is welcome to come for the day and view the gardens, however its invitation only for an extended stay. In fact, during our visit to Gamberaia-Zalum, we were the exclusive guests of the villa. Our apartment, *Nettuno*, was located on the bowling green or Garden Avenue with spectacular views of the gardens, the small town of Settignano, and the city of Florence. At one time this was an indoor ball court for *pallo a corda.* The residence easily accommodates six people with a spacious living room completed by a large antique fireplace and terracotta floors, three double bedrooms, and three bathrooms along with a fully equipped eat-in kitchen. The *Cappella* apartment belonged originally to the villa's 17th century chapel and is also located on the bowling green sharing identical views; readily accommodating six people, its ground floor comprises a large living room with dinning room,

beamed ceilings with terracotta floors, and one double bedroom, bathroom and fully equipped kitchen. The second floor contains two double bedrooms and a bathroom. The *Limonaia* apartment is an historic 15th century farmhouse situated on the upper terrace of the lemon garden. A bit larger, it can accommodate up to eight people with an airy living room with fireplace, beamed ceilings, terracotta floors, a combination kitchen dinning room with an additional fireplace, wall oven and bathroom. The second floor has four double bedrooms, three bathrooms as well as views of the adjacent hills and valleys.

After a morning cappuccino in *la Piazza* of Settignano, we would venture on to explore the neighboring areas. If your timing is right you can experience the *Palio*, an 800-year-old horse race through the streets of Siena, held twice a year in the summer months of July and August, or astound your kids with an up front and personal view of the *leaning Tower of Pisa*. In the late afternoon return to Villa Gamberaia-Zulum for a refreshing swim in the private swimming pool, looking out above the city of Florence. Each evening we dinned out-of-doors on the bowling green, with a view of the *nymphaeum* with Neptune at the north end and the sun setting over Florence to south.

Main garden

Villa Petrischio

Owners/Managers: Isabella and Domenico Tosato and sons Stefano & Giorgio
Via del Petrischio, 25 / Farneta, Cortona (Arezzo) / Italy
Telephone: ++390575610316 / Fax: ++390575610316
E-Mail: villapetrischio@iol.it / Website: www.villapetrischio.it

★★★★ **Price Guide:** €140–€195 • Major credit cards accepted: no American Express **Amenities:** Air conditioning • Bar • Cable/Satellite TV • Internet • Airports: Florence, Rome • Nearby towns: Arezzo, Cortona, Florence, Montalcino, Montepulciano, Perugia, Pienza, and Siena • Restaurant: Breakfast included; lunch & dinner available upon request • Total rooms: 13, plus suites **Activities:** Biking • Children's park • Lake Trasimeno • Golf: 50 km, Circolo Golf Perugia; 55 km, Golf Club Lamborghini • Horseback riding • Shopping: antiques and top designer outlets such as Prada and Gucci • Swimming pool • Termé: Bagno Vignoni • Cultural tours arranged • Water park: Crocodile **Additional Information:** 10% discount in low season

Villa Petrischio is an elegant and exclusive small hotel, positioned at the pinnacle of the highest hill of the area, with the most spectacular views of Val di Chiana. It is located between Tuscany and Umbria which places you in a prime position to visit the best of both regions. It is situated within a short drive to the towns of Cortona, Siena, Arezzo, Florence, Perugia, Pienza, Montalcino, and Montepulciano. The close proximity of the *Autostrada* (highway) permits you to take advantage of nearby sites, returning each afternoon to a sprawling six-acre park of cypresses and pines. Enjoy your special dinner prepared by Villa Petrischio's chef aside the swimming pool while the children cavort in the water and play on the swings. The sunset provides a magnificent backdrop when accompanied by a delectable bottle of regional wine.

Villa Petrischio has been in Isabella's family for one hundred years and was originally owned by her great-grandfather, Berti Guastini. She, along with her husband Domenico and their sons, Stefano and Giorgio, have maintained strong ancestral roots. Their innovative architectural ideas have created a holiday home with modern comforts and original 18th century design. When the house was restored thirty-five years ago, the red brick arches that separate the main room of the ground floor were extended creating a large living room where you can relax amongst the fireplace, wood-beam ceilings, and 19th Century Tuscan furniture. Thirteen bedrooms and suites overlook the park and can accommodate twenty-six guests. The villa and adjacent 18th Century house has a total of four suites. For celebrations and private ceremonies, there is an ancient chapel. Dinners in the main villa as well as large receptions in the park or by the swimming pool can be arranged.

Villa Petrischio is a home for all seasons. Isabella tells me that each Christmas the same extended family occupies the entire villa. A specialized banquet is prepared for their holiday feast. Afterwards, the relatives exchange gifts. On New Year's Eve, the Tosato's arrange live music and dinner, followed by poolside fireworks over the valley. In mid-August, the celebration of Ferragosto is a popular time for an Italian holiday excursion.

This particularly safe and relaxed environment was where we welcomed David's brother Pete and our sister-in-law Helene with their two children, Lauren (nine), and Jason (five). This was their maiden voyage out of the United States. We were intent to bring them into familiar surroundings and comforts to ease the beginning of their Italian vacation. The secure enclosed land of this Tuscan country home accomplished this.

Villa Rigacci Hotel

Owner: Pierazzi family
Localitá Vaggio, 50066 / Reggello, Firenza (Florence) / Italy
Telephone: ++390558656718/8656562 / Fax: ++390558656537
E-Mail: hotel@villarigacci.it / Web: www.villarigacci.com

★★★★ **Price Guide:** €99–€160 double • Major credit cards accepted **Amenities:** Air conditioning • Babysitting: arranged in advance • Bar • Cable/Satellite TV • Airport: Florence • Nearby towns: Arrezzo, Florence, and Siena • Restaurant: includes breakfast; lunch & dinner à la carte • Total rooms: 27 **Activities:** Swimming pool: children's area **Additional Information:** Car necessary; rentals can be arranged • Children 4-18: additional bed €15/superior room, €10/double; cots free • Half board/full board

In the sixteen acres of parks and gardens that surround this 15th century villa, we enjoyed the company of our special friends from Atlanta, the Brusack's. This was Jerry's, Kim's, and their sixteen year-old daughter Heather's first sojourn to Italy as a family. Jerry had journeyed solo in past years, but traveling with a teenage daughter brought "fresh" perspective to the experience. Prior to our rendezvous, they were touring France while we explored other regions of Italy,

yet the timing was perfect. We were all ready to expand our family circles. Uniting with others changes the dynamics through the addition of brand new viewpoints.

If you are searching for a fitting location to gather with friends and family, Villa Ragicci has much to offer: Twenty-seven bedrooms ranging from standard, double, superior double, or suites, the latter of which I would suggest for your families. Villa Ragicci is also within easy reach by both car and train to Arezzo, Florence, and Siena. On a spacious terrace alongside the swimming pool that contains a children's area inclusive of a stone fountain, we spent pleasurable moments relaxing and relishing our time together. The convenience of the poolside bar contributed to a no-hassle vacation. Additionally, Ristorante "Le Vieux Pressoir" serves breakfast, lunch, or dinner in their attractive dining room or outside overlooking the hills and valleys. Our families feasted upon well-prepared regional cuisine accompanied by delectable wines, ending with creative desserts, all canopied under the moonlit Tuscan skies.

Subsequently, our next stop with the Brusacks was a villa on the outskirts of Cortona. The directions were obscure to begin with since they were David's interpretation from a conversation that had transpired completely in Italian. As familiar as we were with Cortona, we found this difficult. Exceedingly so! For over two hours, our car's entourage increased each time we stopped to ask for directions. Italians have many virtues such as warmth, hospitality, and kindness so,

nonetheless, each person insisted that he was the best acquainted with the precise location of this property. Repeatedly, they would motion our cars to pull over, conferring on the next administrative decision. All the men from each car, six in attendance, including David and Jerry, stood at the intersections, hands motioning in every direction. At one point, I enthusiastically ran to Kim conveying the fact that Italians have certain hand gestures to communicate feelings and thoughts. As her eyes gazed in their direction, one of the men reached down to scratch himself. By this point, we were all so euphoric with laughter, finding the villa was secondary to the road there. Our counsel assembled back into their respective cars. Further along, as we approached yet another intersection, two cars were waving us along. Suddenly, and with synchronicity, everyone came to a halting stop. The people parked up ahead were the owners of our long-lost villa. They were waiting to escort us to our Tuscan farmhouse set amidst a field of sunflowers with endless hiking paths.

Castello Dell'Oscano

Owner: Maurizio Bussolati
Strada della Forcella, 37 / Cenerente - Perugia / Italy
Tel. ++39 75690125 / Fax ++39 75690666
E-Mail:Info@oscano.it / Reservations: reservation@oscano.com / Web: www.oscano.it

★★★★ **Price guide:** €150–€275 • Major credit cards accepted **Amenities:** Air conditioning • Baby sitting: on request • Bar • Cable/Satellite TV • Internet • Laundry • Airports: Rome and Florence • Nearby towns: Perugia, Gubbio, and Arezzo • Restaurant: includes breakfast; lunch & dinner à la carte • Total rooms: Castle: 11 rooms & suites; Villa Ada: 22; La Macina: 13 apartments **Activities:** Mountain Biking • Park • Small fishing lake • Golf: 10 km Antognolla Golf and Country Club • Gym • Hiking • Horseback riding • Shopping: Specialty of Perugia; chocolate • Swimming pool • Tennis court • Cultural tours **Additional Information:** Ping Pong • Rental car reservations • 5,000 examples of olive trees • 200 Umbrian wines • Cooking lessons • Half board/full board

Castello dell' Oscano summons you to, "…come and pay us a visit, whether for work and negotiations or to relax, chat, and enjoy yourself with your friends. Devote yourself to your favorite sports, or celebrate that very special occasion." The Oscano residences, which are comprised of the Castle, Villa Ada, and La Macina dell' Oscano (also known as The Oscano Mill) are impeccably situated amid a wooden hillside with fleeting views of the Umbrian valley.

The castle is a large, fortified epoch residence, complete with four crowned towers that comprise rooms available for lodging during your stay. On hand for your dining pleasure is a private canopied gazebo. The remainder of the rooms are decorated with unpretentious refinement, embellished with antique furniture, and equipped with modern comforts. Next to the Castello is the Villa Ada with its elegant cozy rooms. Here you have access to the sitting rooms and the library, which is an ideal atmosphere for relaxing as a family. 'La Macina dell' Oscano' is a farm holiday compound below the castle. These are small, self-contained apartments with cooking amenities. It is surrounded by 250 *hectares* (.40 = 1 acre) of park, which includes the swimming pool for all of Castello dell' Oscano. This farming estate offers a relaxed natural setting with expedient access to all the opulence of the castle and Villa Ada. Whichever accommodation you choose while at Castello dell' Oscano, a flawless welcome awaits your family.

The facility also includes mountain biking, swimming, and sports activities. David and Isaac spent an afternoon golfing nearby and came back raving about Golf Club Antognolla, a Robert

Trent Jones course in the Umbrian hills. For additional information call ++39 075 6059562 or contact info@antognolla.com. David advises that if you are serious about your game, bring your own clubs.

This incredible wooded countryside is just minutes from Perugia, one of the most bustling cities of central Italy, and a classic Italian hill town overlooking the Tiber River Valley. Along with producing some of Italy's best chocolates, there is Piazza IV Novembre, which is the center of the art district. Mussolini founded the University of Perugia and the Italian University for Foreigners that heightened Perugia's already cultural appeal.

The 'Ristorante Turandot' is located within the castle. My kids described the outstanding lunch the three of them shared on the terrace overlooking the valley, a lunch comprised of large plates of *Mozzarella Di Bufala*, fresh tomatoes, basil, bread, butter, and cheese. It wasn't so much what they ate but the superb service and kindness extended to them as kids.

Castello dell' Oscano's restaurant brings into being a style of service reflective of the mid-19th century. A prefixed menu is served each evening connected to Umbria's long established procedures and fresh accessible produce. Although dinner jackets are not required, the manner in which we dressed was a casual elegance. Oscano's wine list is extensive, housing over two hundred local types in their ancient cellar. Their chef will teach cooking classes in the traditional methods. November through January is *brucatura,* when the olives are picked and developed into oil from their olive trees. This is a chance to taste the fresh, rich, olive oil produced by diverse types of olives.

The atmosphere of utter tranquility and warmth joined by the magic of its natural surroundings makes the Castello dell`Oscano an ideal choice for your Italian family holiday. The management will be pleased to accommodate your every need.

❧ *David on Golf* ❧

Think about it. The soil is dark and rich. The sun shines bright and the mountain air is fresh and cool. Italy produces some of the best wine and olives in the world. So I ask you, do you think they can grow some grass if they want? You bet they can. As a matter of fact, I have played many of the best golf courses in America, but Italy can rival any of them.

I love to golf, and I'm blessed because I have a live-in foursome with Jacob, Isaac and Ari. When in the Perugia area, I would encourage you to play a new golf course called Golf Club Antognolla. It is only about a fifteen-minute ride from the Castello dell' Oscano (Central Italy). The setting of this course is like nothing I have ever seen before. What makes it so unique is that it is located in a valley surrounded by mountains. Overlooking the course is an uninhabited medieval city that is presently being restored as a future hotel, residential, and commercial property.

Isaac and I played this golf course in the late afternoon. The fairways and greens were near perfect. They reminded me of the rye grass that you see at Georgia's Augusta National (where the Masters is played), which produce a perfect lie and yield great divots. The greens were soft and spongy, yet they had some speed to them. I actually could back the ball up. I really liked that the course was wide open. Most of our tee-shots were from elevated tee areas and the mountain backdrops gave great contrast so you could watch your ball fly through the air. It was an easy course to walk, and the green fees were very reasonable.

Isaac and I both played with rented clubs. They were probably ten years old and were not of the best quality, but we still had a wonderful day of golf—so don't feel that you have to pack your clubs in order to play.

Hotel Palazzo Piccolomini

Manager: Roberto Mazzolae
Piazza Ranieri 36 / Orvieto 05018 / Italy
Telephone: ++390763341743 / Fax: ++390763391046
E-Mail: Piccolomini.hotel@orvienet.it / Web: www.hotelpiccolomini.it

★★★★ **Price Guide:** €138–€227 **Amenities:** Air conditioning • Bar • Cable/Satellite TV • Internet • Airport: Florence • Closest towns: Orvieto and Arezzo • No restaurant: Breakfast included • Total rooms: 32; 22 doubles, 7 singles and 3 suites **Activities:** • Golf: nearby • Horseback riding: nearby • Shopping

In February of 1999, we were traversing the streets of Orvieto in pursuit of lodging. Although the kids were tired from a full day of excursions, it didn't interfere with our scrutinizing routine of hotel selection. In the center of Piazza Ranieri stood the 16th century restored palace. Originally built for the Pontifical family, Hotel Palazzo Piccolomini is a pre-existing medieval structure that was scrupulously restored in 1991. Orvieto's Etruscan roots are evident in Palazzo Piccolomini's underground area. Your kids will be amazed to discover how this city ascends from below the earth. Its historical splendor co-exists with a fashionable décor producing a high quality four-star hotel.

We loved Palazzo Piccolomini's location. Here you can easily access the Duomo, Piazza Della Repubblica, and the multitudinous shops, bars, and great Umbrian restaurants. An effortless drive from town positions you to visit many of the attractive villages of Umbria and Tuscany.

Hotel Palazzo Piccolomini has three suites, twenty-two double rooms, and seven single rooms with air-conditioning, TV, mini-bar, and hair-dryer. They have their own private parking, wine cellar, and café; however, what is most outstanding is their attentive service. Assisting us with dinner plans took on a new meaning when Roberto, the manager, personally escorted us to the restaurant and remained until we were seated. We have, and will continue to return, to this little palace for a guaranteed pleasurable stay.

Villa Di Piazzano

Owners: The Wimpole Family
Manager: Alessandra Wimpole
Localita` Piazzano / 06069 Tuoro sul Trasimeno (PG)
Tel: ++39 075 826226 / Fax: ++39 075 826336
E-mail: info@villadipiazzano.com / Website: www.villadipiazzano.com

★★★★ **Price Guide:** €150–€225, Breakfast included • Major credit cards accepted • Airport: Florence's Amerigo Vespucci International Airport • Nearby Towns: Cortona 4km • Borders of Umbria and Tuscany actually runs across the property • Assisi, Montepulciano, Lake Trasimeno, and Perugia are close by **Amenities:** 14 spacious and attractive rooms with 1-suite • Parking • Air Conditioning • baby sitting on request • bathroom with hair drier and towel warmer • elevator • Mini-bar • Bar • Currency exchange • Color and Satellite TV • Safe • Telephone • Restaurant: meals by request • Meeting rooms with 20 seats • Non-smoking rooms • Formal gardens with swimming pool **Activities:** Tennis 5km • Golf 20km • Horse riding 5km • Bicycle rentals • walking and jogging trails **Additional information:** The Villa di Piazzano is eager to tailor excursions and activities according to the needs of the individuals and small groups • Minimum stay: 2 nights • Small pets allowed

Villa di Piazzano stands as nobly as its powerful history. Silvio Passerini, Cardinal of Cortona, built the Villa di Piazzano in the early 1500's as his summer hunting manor. Past accounts indicate that the Cardinal was taken under the wing of the influential Florentine Medici family after his father, Rosado, was imprisoned for overtly supporting the causes of the Medici's. While Silvio Passerini was brought up and educated by Lorenzo De Medici, he became especially close to Giovanni, for whom he exhibited his greatest allegiance. Silvio followed Giovanni to the battlefront in France where they fought alongside each other and were both imprisoned. When Giovanni became Pope Leo X, he made Silvio Passerini both Cardinal and Bishop of Cortona, passing on to him some of the controls that beforehand had been given only to the dioceses of Florence and Arezzo; furthermore, Silvio Passerini's position of power contributed to the improvement of the city of Cortona, in addition to some of its main buildings. Today, directly behind the villa in the same hills that the cardinal went hunting is the location of the historical Battles of Trasimeno, and centuries earlier, between Hannibal and the Romans just eighteen kilometers away in Sanguineto.

In the present day the Villa di Piazzano has been completely renovated and modernized into a refined country residence, providing a relaxed as well as elegant ambiance, adorned with a graceful intermingling of the wimpole families' antiques and up-to-the-minute amenities. Each bedroom's décor is distinctive with remarkable views of the hills, ancient gardens of oak and linden tees, the surrounding fields of Piazzano's grape vineyards and olive trees, or the close by town of Cortona. The Winpole family achieved this exceptional blend by remaining committed to safeguarding the original splendor and authenticity of the manor house.

Gracious hospitality, accompanied by attention to fine details, comes both naturally and through experience to the Winpole family who represents five generations of innkeepers. In fact, Villa di Piazzano is home to Alessandra's precocious two-year-old daughter Lisa, who is most ingratiating and will converse with you in both Italian and English.

Villa di Piazzano is ideally situated bordering both the green undulating hills of Umbria, and the enchanting region of Tuscany, with its medieval villages renowned for their history, art, and tradition. Many fascinating towns like Arezzo, Assisi, Chianti, Deruta, Gubbio, Lake Trasi-

meno, Montepulciano, and Perugia are close enough to allow for great day trips. Of course wineries and olive oil mills abound in this most fertile area.

Truthfully, once we were settled in at Villa di Piazzano, we didn't feel the need to leave, except to eat. The sizeable swimming pool with its outstanding landscape, and most restful lounge chairs, was ideal. Jacob and Isaac explored the area by bicycle while Ari swam and played soccer with some new friends. That seemed to follow suite for most of the other guests as well. The range of visitors was diverse such as a family from England with two young kids, mother and her chef daughter exploring cooking classes in Tuscany, honeymooners, and an American family celebrating a collage graduation. Actually, we often joined other families in experiencing different locale restaurants. Everyone was friendly and excited to share his or her favorite spots. One evening we dinned at the Villa, enjoying a traditional preset home cooked meal, accompanied by their own fine Merlot wine and olive oil, which was a pleasant ending to a peaceful day.

Castello Chiola Dimora Storica

Manager: Luciano Di Battista
Via Degli Aquino, 12 / 65014 Loreto Aprutino, Pescara (Abruzzo) / Italy
Telephone: ++39 085 8290690 / Fax: ++39 085 8290677
E-Mail: castellochiola@hotmail.com / Web: www.pregiohotel.com\chiola.htm

★★★★ **Price Guide:** €155–€240 • Major Credit Cards accepted **Amenities:** Four-Star • Air conditioning • Baby sitting • Bar • TV • Internet • Laundry • Nearby airports are Abruzzo • Nearest town is Pescara • Restaurant. Breakfast included. • Total number of rooms - 36 **Activities:** Golf, 18km • Horseback riding • Private Beach nearby • Swimming pool • Terme Carsmanico, 40km towards Rome • Tours of vineyards and cities • Water park, Aqua Splash **Additional Information:** August 15, ghost party with dinner at the swimming pool. • Additional bed, €26.

The majestic Castello Chiola emerges from the hilltop of the medieval town of Loreto Aprutino. Now a grand hotel, it was originally built in the 19th century C.E. During the following centuries many noble families owned the castle. Although the castle was not involved in central historical milestones, it did encounter many important events: King Charles V stayed in this castle around the 1st century of the 2nd millennium before crowning his son king of Italy in the ancient nearby Roman town of Penne. It's hearsay that in 1239 Saint Thomas Aquinas maintained residence here and performed the notorious "miracle of the roses." The last owners, the Chiola family, resided here from the last decades of the 19th century to 1995 when the castle was restored and converted into a stately hotel, maintaining their family name.

Abruzzo, one of Europe's greenest areas, is a region well suited for adventurous outdoor activity throughout the seasons. Enjoy a horseback ride, mountain bike, hike, or cross-country ski within an environmentally protected region. This area extends from Gran Sasso, among mountains which are home to wolf and bear, the hills of vineyards and olive trees, as well as the beaches of the Adriatic. If golf is "your bag," the hotel will arrange a shuttle service to a course thirty minutes away. It is just a twenty-five minute car ride to the sea where the concierge will reserve beach chairs and umbrellas for your family's relaxation during the summer months.

Emerging from the land's rich soil and the sea is a distinctive cuisine. Most recently, Loreto Aprutino's olive oil was recognized for producing the best olive oil in Italy: *Olio D.O.P.* We mentioned to our waiter that we had heard their olive oil to be infamous which resulted in a personal olive oil tasting. The five of us nearly consumed an entire bottle, dipping bread into this fragrant liquid gold, leaving minimal room for the rest of the meal.

The rooms in the Castello are all very large and spacious. The kids shared a regally decorated triple room. We had a double room offering us a stunning view over the pool and valley below. The manager, Luciano Di Battista, required no encouragement in the area of welcoming the Levinson family travelers to his hotel. Castello Chiola had a hospitable atmosphere and was a great home base for exploring Abruzzo's multi-faceted geological environment.

Albergo Del Sole Al Pantheon

Manager: Giancarlo Piraino
Piazza della Rotonda, 63 / Rome 00186, Italy
Telephone: ++39 066 780441 / Fax: ++39 066 780441
E-Mail: info@hotelsolealpantheon.com / Web: www.hotelsolealpantheon.com/welcome.htm

★★★★ **Price Guide:** €290–€460 • Major Credit Cards accepted **Amenities:** Air conditioning • Baby sitting • Bar • TV • Internet • Laundry • Nearby airport is Rome, 30 minutes • Nearest town is Rome • No Restaurant. Breakfast is included. • Total number of rooms – 31, 7 apartments, 3 junior suites **Activities:** Shopping, extensive selection of everything made in Italy • Cultural and historic tours with English guide or any requested language **Additional Information:** Located in the historic center of Rome, in the square of the Pantheon

The area around the Pantheon has always been considered the heart of Roman hospitality. Standing in Piazza Della Rotonda, a hotel ancient as the ground it is built on, Albergo Del Sole Al Pantheon dates back to 1467 when it was known as *Locanda del Montone* (The Ram Inn). Resplendent restoration has brought back its original grandeur.

The Sole Al Pantheon has remained loyal to its calling, that of a gracious inn. Many illustrious guests throughout the centuries have lodged here, from Emperor Frederic III Hapsburg, poet Ludovico Ariosto, whose verses from the *Fourth Satire* are engraved on a marble slab and can be read on the facade, and Jean Paul Sartre who along with Simone de Beauvoir were regular guests. Albergo Del Sole's location is my favorite location in which to explore this multi-faceted, cultural, gastronomic, and fashion capital. The concierge is quick to arrange limousine services, city tours, and excursions to surrounding areas. Personally, we most appreciate the ability to walk, knowing we can take the occasional taxi or bus if needed. Any direction you choose to take puts you face-to-face with the greatest historical edifices in the world: Piazza Venezia, where the Venetian Cardinal Pietro Barbo built his family's summer residence; Palazzo Venezia, the first grand example of Roman renaissance architecture; Piazza Navona, surrounded by aristocratic palaces demonstrating Roman baroque architecture and has, for centuries, been the heart of social life; *Piazza Di Spagno* (the Spanish Steps), with its beautiful stairway connecting the square to the church of Trinitá del Monte which the French built while vying for supremacy over the Spaniards; the *Fontana della Barcaccia* (boat fountain) built by Pietro Bernini at the foot of the Spanish Steps; *Fontana Di Trevi* (Trevi Fountain), the most famous fountain in Rome, celebrates the reactivation of the ancient Roman aqueducts, animated by sheer cliffs, tritons, sea-creatures, and water falls; and Piazza Del Popolo, where Guiseppe Valadier combined baroque architecture and integrated nature, and which sits next to Villa Borghese, Rome's largest public garden.

A ten-minute walk placed us in the Jewish ghetto where our family was welcomed for an evening service after Isaac identified our heritage at the gate with a quick Jewish prayer. We then joined some special Roman friends at the "Kosher Bistrot." During our stay, we regularly treated ourselves to *Gelato di Roma* at Caffé La Palma for an overwhelming assortment of sensational ice cream and chocolate.

Each evening we returned home to the intimacy of Albergo Del Sole. As I peered out my arched-shaped open window and witnessed lively cafés, lovers caressing, and the Pantheon, I felt the impact of centuries past and the present day magic of Roma.

Country Relais I Due Laghi

Director: Nizza Family / Director: Mateo Marzano
Localitá Le Cerque / I-00061 Anguillara Sabazia (Roma) / Italy
Telephone: ++390699607059 / Fax: ++390699607068
E-Mail: info@iduelaghi.it / Web: www.iduelaghi.it

★★★★ **Price guide:** €150–€253 • Major credit cards accepted **Amenities:** Air conditioning • Babysitting • Bar • Cable/Satellite TV • Laundry • Airport: Rome 50 km • Nearby towns: Rome, Viterbo, Maglianos, Civitavecchia, Anguillara • Restaurant: Breakfast included; lunch & dinner à la carte • Total rooms: 32 **Activities:** Biking • Boat rentals: motor, wind surfing, sailing, & canoe trips. • Children's park • Fishing • Golf: 20 km at Oigiata and Sutri • Hiking • Horse back riding • Massage, specifically Shiatsu • Beach on the lake • Swimming pool • Tennis court • Cultural tours **Additional information:** Open all year • Meeting facilities • Half board/full board

In this tranquil yet refined atmosphere, the emphasis is on comfort. Mateo Marzano is the manager of I Due Laghi, which derives its name from the location between the two Roman lakes of Braciano and Martignano. Mr. Marzano has an embracing personality that warmly welcomes you into his estate. He recognizes that when you arrive by plane and car, you are tired and in need of rest. Reflecting back to the 3rd century B.C.E., when travelers arrived by foot or horse and carriage on the same road, via Cassian way, customer satisfaction is as important to him and his staff today as in bygone years. He says, "If you leave unhappy, we did not deliver our Italian-made hospitality." Mr. Marzano is confident in their hotel's ability to accomplish this because of its diminutive size. He says this allows them to be in touch with the needs of all of their guests. He is eager and devoted to sharing the historical richness of this area, dating back to the 11th century.

Lake Braciano is the result of a volcanic eruption. The old medieval village of Anguillara Sabazia was an important fortified village. In recent decades, Anguillara has become a favorable destination of the Romans, as the summer offers many attractions. Lake Braciano is less than 30 kilometers from Rome. Either by car or train, you are promptly in the heart of the Eternal City; however, choose to spend the day at I Due Laghi, and you will discover an abundance of activities to enjoy while the sun is still above the horizon. On the lake, Italian championship regattas have taken place for many years. There are sailing schools and yacht clubs, with boat and wind surfboard rentals readily available. Lake

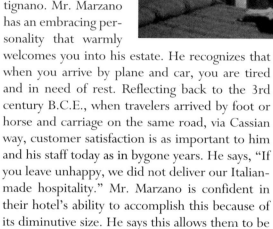

Braciano's uncontaminated water allowed for trout breeding, making fishing prime.

I Due Laghi offers tennis and bicycle riding. Its swimming pool is set in a peaceful garden, with a casual snack bar close by. An equestrian club is situated on the estate, offering skilled horse riders lessons and excursions. They also organize drag hunt at regular intervals of which Mr. Marzano is an expert. A Drag Hunt is similar in nature to a fast cross country horse ride. The hounds do not chase a live quarry, instead an artificial scent, "the drag" is laid by a lead horse over a distance of approximately three to four miles.

One of the first and most important historical aeronautic museums in Europe is located in this area. The collection is unique including a wooden reproduction of a flying machine with a ladder to get on and off, originally designed by Leonardo da Vinci. Your stay in Anguillara Sabazia can only be completed by a tour of Castello Odescalchi with its significant collection of medieval arms. We visited with my five-year-old nephew, Jason; hence, my recommendation is to ensure that your guide is speaking only in your native language. Do an abbreviated visit to the rooms that hold particular interest to your children. Everyone enjoyed the panoramic tour of the patrol area, which links together the six towers of the castle.

This rustic style country relais has twenty-five rooms and seven suites. The restaurant, La Posta dé Cavalieri, is known for serving fresh home-made products. In fact, you can purchase fresh *formaggio e ricotta* (ricotta cheese) directly from them. While dining, as is prevalent throughout I Due Laghi, dress for comfort.

Grand Hotel Parco Dei Principi

General Manager: Carla Milos
000198 Roma Via G. Frescobaldi, 5 / Rome, Italy
Telephone: ++3906854421 / Fax: ++39068845104 / Fax: Reservation: ++39 06 8551758
E-Mail: principi@parcodeiprincipi.com / Web: www.parcodeiprincipi.com

★★★★★ **Price guide:** €540–€750/per night, Presidential and royal suites on request • Major credit cards accepted **Amenities:** Air conditioning • Babysitting • Bar • Cable/Satellite TV • Internet • Laundry • Airport: Rome • Nearby town: Rome • Restaurant: Breakfast included; lunch & dinner à la carte. • Total rooms: 180, 30 suites. **Activities:** Biking • Park • Gym • Massage: by appointment • Shopping: high fashion • Swimming pool • Cultural tours **Additional Information:** Meeting facilities: 500 people • Parking: €21 • Piano bar

At 9:00 p.m., the kids were exhausted from our drive up from the Amalfi coast. We arrived at our intended accommodation whose appearance was closer to a brothel than a hotel. With one glance at my expression, the boys knew Mom was not going to spend her final evening of our trip here. David, in his unwavering ability to make the best of the situation said, "It is just a place to sleep. We are leaving in 12 hours anyway." For me it is all the more reason to create the idyllic circumstances.

My perseverance settled us among the lush surroundings of the Grand Hotel Parco Dei Principi. Hospitality is their calling. Carla Milos is the general manager, and he is there to instill the philosophy that your "every wish is fulfilled, every command obeyed." In the heart of Rome, surrounded by sensational botanical gardens, Parco Dei Principi looks out onto the eminent Villa Borghese, Rome's largest public garden. This location provides convenient access to some of the best-known sites within a tranquil paradise. Lounging at the swimming pool enveloped by the rich vegetation will delight the soul. The hotel's conviction to do the utmost in their quest to create an efficient congenial ambiance was apparent upon arriving. The attentiveness to our family's needs was delightfully overwhelming. Without an utterance, they evaluated our situation, ushering us to the upgraded "royal suite." We occupied three bedrooms and two full bathrooms, equipped with every possible amenity. The tone

of our last night in the eternal city was transformed on the spot.

After we all took long luxurious Jacuzzi baths, we relaxed in our robes and slippers and dressed for one of the most remarkable dinners we had experienced in Rome. The concierge had called ahead to Capricios. Immediately seated, we then experienced an endless sea of food and wine: imaginative salads and *antipasti*, regional Lazio pasta, fish, meat, chicken, breads, fresh bufalo mozzarella and ricotta cheeses, desserts, *grappes*, and *espresso*. A hedonistic banquet to seduce the most resistive appetites. My boys were absorbed by the drama of this unique dining extravaganza while, for David and I, it reinforced our love, lust, and desire to further immerse our lives in this intriguing culture.

Hotel Adriano Ristorante

Owner: Cinelli family
Adriana, 194 / Tivoli–Villa Adriana (Rome) 00010 / Italy
Telephone: ++39 0774 53502 / Or 382235 / Fax: ++39 0774 535122
E-Mail: info@hoteladriano.it / Web: www.hoteladriano.it

★★★ **Price guide:** €113-€196 • Major credit cards accepted **Amenities:** Air conditioning • Cable/Satellite TV • Laundry • Restaurant: Breakfast included; lunch & dinner à la carte • Total rooms: 10, including 3 junior suites & 2 singles **Activities:** Swimming pool: nearby • Terme`: Bagni d' Tivoli **Additional Information:** Tours: Villa d' Este, and Hadrian's Villa • Parking

Hotel Adriano Ristorante sits amidst a garden at the entrance to Hadrians Villa, which was built during the first ten years of Emperor Hadrian's rule. The set of buildings are of immense character, extending over 120 *hectares* (.40 = 1 acre) of outstanding landscape. Nearby is the Villa D' Este with some of the most extraordinary and magnificent assembly of terraced gardens, sculptures, fountains, pools, and Neapolitan architecture. Your kids will be awed by the ability of the fountains to be propelled solely by gravity.

This is an area on the outskirts of Rome, which is often mistakenly overlooked. Tivoli is a small modest town, which borders the lower slopes of the Apennines Mountains and was an important holiday resort. Still existing are the ancient *terme* (baths) and the *Teatro Marittimo* (marine theater).

Hotel Adriano Ristorante is a charming bed and breakfast with outstanding gourmet cuisine. My kids were so inspired by the artful presentation of food they photographed the display. This was one of their first encounters with the Roman, hedonistic style of life. The rooms are handsomely decorated, but the draw to Adriano is truly their inspiring culinary flair. With kids, this is a great one-night stand. *Buon Appetito!*

David Keeps Smiling

In the back of my mind, I remember someone telling me the one thing you don't want to do is have to go to the dentist in Italy. So we always make a point to have our scheduled dental check-ups before we leave for vacation. Sometimes the best made plans will still backfire because of unpredictable circumstances.

It was two days before we were to leave Rome when I had the unpleasant experience of having some type of food get lodged in between my tooth and gum. It quickly swelled and became inflamed. I developed an excruciating toothache and was miserable. I felt like I had no choice but to get to a dentist, so I spoke to a close friend in the medical community and was referred to his personal dentist. I was nervous about seeing a dentist who I was unfamiliar with; however, because of the severity of the pain, I had no choice.

The dentist was located in a fashionable part of town, just off of the Via Veneto in Rome. His office was in a professional building that looked like it was once a royal palace. There was a large iron gate, which led into a courtyard. Once in the building, there was an antique elevator and marble staircase that took me to the office suites, located on the upper floors. When I entered the office, I could tell that there was a huge gap in the dental technology of Italy compared to that of the United States. It reminded me of the dental office that I went to in the 1960's when I was a child.

When I was escorted to the exam room, I was shocked that the room was about 12x12 and had an office partition dividing it into two halves. There was another patient being treated in the same room. It wasn't but a few minutes later that I realized how lucky I was to be sharing the room. My first interaction with a professional in this office was with a dental assistant who spoke no English. So when she started to speak to me, I couldn't completely understand what she was saying. Finally, I heard the gentleman who was sharing the room with me and who evidently also had tools and fingers in his mouth mumble to me. "She wants you to open your mouth and point to where it hurts." At this point I didn't know whether to laugh or cry. Here I am in pain, in a foreign country, with a non-English speaking dental assistant, and taking instruction from a patient who is also being treated in the same room, at the same time.

Moments later, the dentist came into the room who, fortunately, spoke English and began chastising the assistant in a joking manner for the way she was handling me. He then tells me to open my mouth and the first thing he says is, "Oh no, not good. The tooth is bad and I think we may need to take it out." In three seconds, I'm sweating and thinking. I am forty-five years old, I have been brushing my teeth three times a day and flossing after every meal, I still have every tooth God gave me and, in a five-second exam, this dentist decides that he is going to pull my tooth. I'm thinking, get me out of here. Well, the good news was that the dentist found out we were scheduled to leave in 48 hours, and he didn't feel like it was wise to operate under those circumstances. The bad news is what he elected to do. Moments later, he started doing a root planning of the tooth. Did I mention that he did this without any anesthesia or Novocain? I can't describe, in words, what the pain felt like. Let it suffice to say it hurt. I walked out of the office in more pain than when I walked in. The good news was that a few hours later, I was pain-free, and the swelling and the problem were totally gone.

Hotel Lord Byron

Owner: Sig. Amedeo Ottaviani
General Manager: Andrea L. Luri
Via G. De Notaris 5-00197 / Rome, Italy
Telephone: ++39 063220404 / Fax: ++ 39 063220405
E-mail: info@lordbyronhotel.com / Website: www.lordbyronhotel.com

★★★★★ **Price Guide:** €350-€950 per room/per day, includes generous buffet breakfast • Major credit cards accepted • Nearest Airport: Rome's Fiumicino • Nearest town: Rome **Amenities:** In the center of Rome • 36 rooms • first floor of the building is comprised of rooms decorated in the art-deco style, while the higher floors consist of suites, each containing stunning white marble baths, complete with towel-warmers and hair-dryers, plus terraces suitable for room service • *The Garden Suite* that is located in a separate building has an independent Roman style atrium and a beautiful terrace great for private meals • Fully air-conditioned • Satellite color television • Multi-lingual staff • Room service • Parking nearby • Limousine airport transfer and privately chauffeured excursions upon request • World renown gourmet restaurant **Sapori** *del Lord Byron:* serving breakfast, lunch, and dinner • *The Cellar:* winner of the "Award of Excellence" by *Wine Spectator* magazine • *Il Salotto* lounge and wine bar **Activities:** Sightseeing • Museums and Shopping • Biking and Jogging in nearby *Borghese Gardens* • Horseback riding and tennis nearby • 18 hole golf course 30 minutes from hotel **Additional Information:** Extra bed available in Double Superior rooms • Junior Suites and Suites • Special offer: For minimum stays of 3 nights, a courtesy airport transfer service in private sedan cars is arranged upon arrival • Complete travel information is needed upon reservation confirmation.

Regally positioned atop a slight prominence, in the exclusive *Parioli* quarter of Rome, is this impeccable *White House,* known as Hotel Lord Byron. From the moment you walk through the gate, ascend a short flight of stairs, then walk through the glass doors bordered by brass columns, you know that your well-being is of foremost importance. All the rooms and suites are tastefully designed bringing forth both splendor and comfort. Every detail has been considered, from the well-designed décor, to the fine linens and exotic flowers. Much of this experience is due to the careful guidance of Amedeo Ottaviani, the sagacious owner of this newly restored illustrious hotel, who has redefined a warm welcome with what he refers to as, *'vintage hospitality.'* The staff of Hotel Lord Byron is always on hand; still they appreciate your need for time alone with your family.

The chefs at the hotel's *Sapori del Lord Byron's* restaurant take pleasure in preparing masterful regional dishes with the true Italian essence. The menu varies every three months in order to utilize only the freshest seasonal ingredients. The ambiance is semi-formal yet the tone is relaxed. We felt at ease to be ourselves, as though we were in the privacy of our own home. No pretentiousness, just sensational food accompanied by quality family time. The kid's most always ordered from the menu, but when Isaac wanted his favorite *Pasta al Pomodoro*, or when Ari preferred his filet mignon which was enveloped by thin slices of eggplant, potatoes and sweet ewe's

cheese au gratin to be cooked well done, or as he learned to say *'ben cotto'*, it was never a problem. The all-encompassing selection of some of Italy's most highly praised wines harmonized well with their prized cuisine. Do save room for dessert, which is always a grand finale.

Hotel Lord Byron's prime location gives you the best of Rome just outside the gates of Villa Borghese's park and gardens, a short walk to the Via Veneto, and Piazza di Spagna, with the opportunity to unwind in an exceptionally peaceful ambiance. Should you choose to be privately chauffeured, the concierge will arrange for the service. We were ready for some exercise and had the best time riding bicycles through Borghese gardens, with a stop at the zoo and the museum of modern art. On a subsequent day we rented canopied three-seated bicycles that deterred the heat of the summer sun and made for a fun excursion through the streets of Rome.

The motto of this distinctive hotel comes as no surprise: *'Hospitality is like a beautiful flower, it needs plenty of care.'*

Hilton Rome Airport

Manager: Serge Ethuin
Via Arturo Ferrarin 2 / Rome Fiumicino 00050 / Italy
Telephone: United States: 1-800-HILTONS / Europe: + 800 44 45 86 67
Italy: 011390665258 / Fax: 011390665256525
E-Mail: Website to "Contact Us" / Web: www.hilton.com

★★★★★ **Price guide:** €454–€1, 394 • Major credit cards accepted **Amenities:** Air conditioning • Babysitting •
Bar • Cable/Satellite TV • Internet • Laundry • Airport: Rome/connected to hotel • Nearby towns: Fiumicino, Ostia,
and Rome • Restaurant: children's menu; room service; Breakfast, lunch & dinner à la carte • Total rooms: 517
Activities: Gym • Shopping: Rome, Ostia • Swimming pool: indoor • Tennis courts **Additional Information:**
Complete services for business travelers • Meeting facilities • Cribs • Hi-chairs • Playpens • Car rental desk • ATM
• Currency exchange • Multi-lingual staff

Ordinarily we would tend to steer you away from big hotel conglomerates; however, the Hilton Rome Airport is the only accommodation located in the entire airport vicinity. It is directly linked to all the terminals of Leonardi da Vinci International Airport and Train Station by way of a moving walkway through a covered pass way.

Beyond this expedient access lies a deluxe four-star resort featuring 517 rooms, including superior executive and adjoining rooms, junior suites, and one-bedroom suites with parlors. It offers a club-room with a personal concierge, including unlimited food and drink service. We highly recommend this additional amenity especially when your kids have hankering, young appetites. The Hilton offers a complimentary shuttle bus or train, which transports you to the city in 20 to 30 minutes. Its two restaurants and bar serve a supple blend of Italian-American cuisine. Both the breakfast and dinner buffet have an expansive array of tasty selections.

The kids especially love the Hilton. When the indoor pool and workout facility joined forces with in-room dinner and a movie, fun happens. This is where we stay on our last night when scheduled for early departure the next morning. Often we have been traveling for three to six weeks and the kids are ready for a shift back to their familiar cultural surroundings. The Hilton helps ease them back through this transformation.

As for me, my eagerness to alter my state of mind is more complex. Walking through the doors of the Hilton signals in my heart that once again I must depart this treasured land. David, sensitive to my reluctance to leave, always arranges one last interlude in Rome: a fanciful dinner for two in Trastevere or by the beaches of Fiumicino. We savor our last moments reminiscing over the weeks past and fantasizing about future journeys to come.

Hotel Villa Del Parco

Owner: Bernardini Family / General Manager: Allessandro Bernardini
Via Nomentana, 110-00-161 / Rome, Italy
Telephone: ++39 06 4423773 / Fax: ++39 06-44237572
E-Mail: info@hotelvilladelparco.it / Web: www.hotelvilladelparco.it

★★★ **Price Guide:** €144-€204 • Major Credit Cards accepted **Amenities:** Air conditioning • Babysitting • Bar • TV • Internet • Laundry • Nearby airport is Rome • Nearest town: Rome. • Restaurant serves breakfast only and snack bar service. • Total number of rooms - 29 **Activities:** Biking • Shopping extensive selection of everything made in Italy • Tours of Roman history and culture **Additional Information:** Garage parking • Room for disabled guests.

For nearly forty years, the hospitality of the Bernardini family has created a delightful atmosphere to enjoy the most renowned sights of Rome. I was immediately impressed that nearly each time that I telephoned in advance of our stay, Allessandro Bernardini, the general manager, would personally answer. Villa del Parco is on the ancient street of Nomentana yet flanked by trees and quaint gardens. Its location is a shopper's haven, being within walking distance from the famous Via Veneto and the Spanish Steps. We found it convenient to catch the bus across the street, which transported us to all of Rome's most renowned sights.

Built in the liberty style of architecture, Villa del Parco resembles a manor country home. Its twenty-nine comfortable rooms offer modern amenities such as satellite TV, mini bar, telephone, heating, and air conditioning. My favorite area of the hotel is the bar-lounge and outdoor garden café. During the summer months, you can enjoy your breakfast *alfresco* and, in the evening, come back at any hour for light meals or snacks. The Bernardini family and their caring staff are always on hand to ensure that your family has a pleasant stay.

La Posta Vecchia

Manager: Barbara Panzera
00055 Palo Laziale / Rome, Italy
Telephone: ++39069949501 / Fax: ++39069949507
E-Mail: info@lapostavecchia.com / Website: www.lapostavecchia.com

★★★★★ **Price Guide:** €440–€1300 • Major credit cards accepted **Amenities:** Air conditioning • Babysitting • Bar • Cable and Satellite TV • Internet • Laundry • Airport: Rome • Nearby towns: Civitavecchia, Fiumicino, Ostia, and Rome • Restaurant: Breakfast included; lunch & dinner à la carte • Total rooms: 19, including double rooms & suites **Activities:** Biking, • Boat rentals: paddle boat • Golf: 40 minute drive to Le Querce Golf Club & Nepi Olgiata Golf Club • Gym: additional fee • Horseback riding: nearby • Massage • Private beach: at the sea • Sauna • Swimming pool: indoors • Tennis court: nearby fitness center • Cultural tours **Additional Information:** Roman museum on location • Secretarial services • Private cars and shuttle service: additional fee • Open: March 19 to November 8

Upon arrival, we received a letter from the then General Manager, Mr. Franco Ottaviana that began, "Welcome Home. The staff at La Posta Vecchia are at your disposal to fulfill your every whim or desire." Mr. Ottaviani is charming and, together with a Yul Brynner appearance, he has a divine smile and gracious ways. Being in his presence is as soothing as the sea which surrounds us. In this extreme opulence, every staff person is understated, giving you the ability to move about the villa as you would your own home. La Posta Vecchia is a place that seduces you to relax. The constant sound of the surf lulls you into a peaceful tranquility. This area of Palo Laziale hosted emperors, monarchs, and popes and, most recently, heads of state, industrial leaders, presidents of the United States, and Hollywood's finest actors and musicians. The service is prompt, and the food is as exceptional as the wine list. To quote *the New York Times*, "You easily succumb to a fantasy that you are the guest of an aristocrat but then, in a manner of speaking, you are." It is unimaginable that this deluxe hotel located in these exclusive seaside surroundings would be top on my kid's list. The boys commented, "Nobody was peering at me, nor waiting to judge whether my behavior was appropriate or not."

La Posta Vecchia is a family resort indeed and just a 20 minute drive from Rome's Fiumicino Airport. Here you overlook the Mediterranean Sea, which is surrounded by a world wildlife foundation park of 125 hectares (.40 = one acre). The sports activities that are available

include an indoor Romanesque-style pool, a private beach, horseback riding among the Etruscan ruins, tennis, golf, biking, and walks through the extensive grounds. The boys particularly enjoyed the paddleboats and sea kayaks which are at your disposal throughout your stay, and there is a lifeguard on hand to assist you as needed. As in most of our choice family resorts, cultural and historical environments are encompassed in its walls. Directly below most of the ground floor is the remains of a Roman villa dating back 2000 years. The small private underground museum has a multitude of collections of Roman remains and mosaic floors of the original villa which once belonged to Julius Caesar.

This is a place where rich noble Romans built villas of unseen luxury as an ideal spot to spend their hot summer months. It was John Paul Getty's meticulous five-year restoration that led to this great archeological find in the 1960's. He collected fine antiques and art works to decorate the villa. In the early 1980's, a Swiss company acquired the villa, along with the art and furnishings. In 1990, La Posta Vecchia was turned into the luxury hotel it is today. All the magnificent collections and traces of Roman history are there for you to enjoy. La Posta Vecchia accommodations range from double standard rooms to their opulent master suites. Each is furnished within is own individual style.

The Medici Suite, with its wall of windows, carries you outside to the expansive view of the sea. This was our royal residence for our time there. It hosts a grand 17th century, Spanish-style bedroom and a separate, large, sitting room with beautiful wood paneling. As you enter the bathroom descend down one of two Carrara marble staircases, which wind around to encompass the marble tub. Draw a bath, indulge in your complimentary Bvlgari products, open a bottle of Italy's finest wine, and ignite the fireplace set before you and yours.

During our stay, we celebrated Isaac's 12th birthday. Isaac became Caesar for the night, thanks to the thoughtfulness of Mr. Ottaviani. Dinner was set at a grand marble table with candelabras at either end. During the entire evening we felt as though we were in a Shakespearian play. Every staff person in the hotel was chosen perfectly for his or her role. Daniele, the primo chef, is top notch, yet humble. He greeted us and announced the special choices for that evening. Between each act, he would reappear to consult with us further as to the scenes that would follow. For the *finale*, he informed us of a special surprise. We were then escorted into the kitchen and watched the behind-the-curtain preparation. Daniele asked us to please return to our seats at this time, indicating the closing act was about to commence. As the five of us began strolling back to our places, the lights dimmed, and the pianist played a classical version of Happy Birthday as Isaac was presented a specially baked and designed cake.

Should you have only three or four days to spend around Rome, this is the ideal choice with outstanding accommodations along the sea, exceptional cuisine, first-rate hospitality, and accessibility to Rome. La Posta Vecchia is truly a celebration of life for anyone wanting to step back in time to a slowed pace, one often absent in today's modern world.

David on Shopping

One day in February, we were walking the streets around the Spanish Steps in Rome. We noticed there were crowds of people lined up waiting to get into different stores. Every store had signs in the window that said "*Sconti* 50%" or "*Saldi*." Then we noticed a line of over a hundred people waiting to get into a particular store named Davide Cenci. As we walked by, we saw the store packed with people. There was a security guard in front of the entrance and, as two or three people would leave the store, he would allow two or three others to enter. Everyone who exited the store was carrying large orange bags that said Davide Cenci Clothing.

We had never heard of the store but figured there had to be great bargains inside. So to the back of the line we went. After about thirty minutes, we were inside. There was organized chaos. On the ground floor, there were men everywhere pulling clothes off of hanging racks and trying on jackets and sweaters and shirts. Next, Deb went upstairs to the women's department. After about an hour of looking around and trying on different things, I went upstairs to try to find her. When I finally worked my way through the maze of clothing and people, I saw Debra at the end of the store standing half-naked trying on a dress. I asked her what she was doing. She responded by saying, "When in Rome, do as the Romans do." I looked around and saw most of the other women were unclothed as well. She walked out of the store with a dress that she continues to wear years later. It was a $1,500 (USD) hand-made dress that she paid $150.00 (USD) for, a real steal.

Park Hotel Villa Grazioli

Director: Rolf J. Rampf
Via Umberto Pavoni, 19 / 00046 Grottaferrata / Roma, Italy
Telephone: ++39069454001 / Fax: ++39069413506
E-Mail: info@villagrazioli.com / Web: www.villagrazioli.com

★★★★ **Price Guide:** €240–€450. • Major credit cards accepted **Amenities:** Air conditioning • Bar • Cable/Satellite TV • Airport: Rome • Nearby towns: Rome, Frascati and Grattaferrata • Restaurant: includes breakfast; lunch & dinner à la carte • Total rooms: 58 **Activities:** Biking: nearby • Golf: nearby • Swimming: nearby • Tennis courts: nearby **Additional Information:** Open all year • Train station: Frascati • Meeting facilities • Culinary classes • Cultural tours

Cardinal Antonio Carafa built Villa Grazioli at the end of the 16th Century. Through its 500-year history, such important families as the Odescalchi's and Borghese's have owned it. Today, Villa Grazioli is an Italian national monument yet enchanting hotel. Still remaining within the Villa are paintings and mural frescoes by prominent artists such as Caracci and Ciampelli. My most beloved fresco is in the hotel's Galleria, where Pannini painted scenes from the "Book of Genesis" and four of the seven "Days of Creation." Watch the expressions on the faces of your family as their eyes engage upon the work of these master artisans.

Villa Grazioli is situated on the Tusculum hill with panoramic views over the eternal city of Rome. Chef Maurizio Morbidelli uses this backdrop with *al fresco* (outdoor) dining in the summer season to present his typical Roman and Mediterranean cuisine. The terrace is open for your dining pleasure for both lunch and dinner. The Acquaviva Restaurant, located on the ground floor of the villa, is open year round.

After a day of cultural sightseeing, we valued coming home to Villa Grazioli's extensive park setting in an atmosphere full of history and art. Immersed in this rural peacefulness above Rome's city lights, we discussed our day's activities. David and I lingered over our wine while the boys ascended to the security of their Villa room, watching television and playing Game Boy.

Rome is called "The Eternal City." It is here that my impression of life becomes immortalized by the Roman and Etruscan ruins, castles, medieval villages, churches, and synagogues adorned by the art and history of two millennia. In Rome and its surrounding provinces, you will discover the heart of Italy. Whichever location around Rome you choose to situate your family, the explorations are endless. Grattaferrata, and its neighboring town of Frascati, permeate with the essence of the natural and artistic wonders of this area.

Park Hotel Villa Grazioli can arrange cultural excursions for your family. Take an adventurous bike ride through the beautiful "Castelli Romani" natural park. Choose between authentic Patrician villas and Palazzos from the 600's. Most of these villas are still privately owned and require a prior reservation of two weeks. Frascati is famous for wine production. Make a tour of Casale Marchese 13th Century manor house vineyards and wine cellars. Their chef will instruct you in how to choose ingredients along with cooking and presentation of the dishes. You may also choose, as we did, to take a guided journey through Villa Grazioli, discovering for yourself the *Arte e Storia* (art and story) and why the Marquis de Sade wrote in his travel diary, "This villa appeared to me as the most elegant of all the villas in Frascati.

You can admire a fresco that represents monochrome arabesques so masterly shadowed that they look real and you feel like touching them." Complete your day with swimming, tennis, or golf at "Villa Alta" sports club where special rates have been arranged for Villa Grazioli guests. Dinner begins at 8:00 p.m., and the hotel will be pleased to arrange in advance a live classical concert for your enjoyment.

Villa Grazioli's main villa has eleven double rooms and two suites. Villa Paggeria and the *Limonaia* (original lemon plant storage) contain forty-five rooms, two of which are designed for handicapped purposes. All bedrooms have a modest décor and are equipped with air conditioning, telephone, mini-bar, and satellite TV. Each bathroom has a hair dryer and towel warmer. The chance to escape your hustle-bustle every day life awaits you atop this most amazing city.

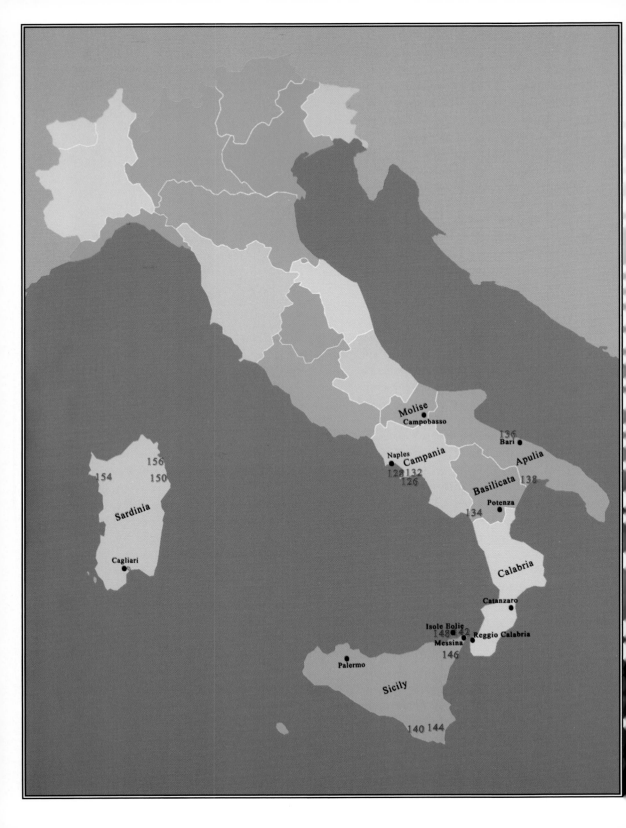

Molise

Campobasso

136
Bari

Naples Campania

Apulia

128 132

126

Basilicata 138

Potenza

134

Sardinia

Cagliari

Calabria

Catanzaro

156

154   150

Isole Eolie

148 142

Reggio Calabria

Messina

146

Palermo

Sicily

140 144

Southern Italy

Sardinian beach at Club Hotel Li Capanni

A secluded grotto off the Aeolian Island of Lipari

Casa Raffaele Conforti

Costiera Amalfitana / Owner: Andrea Cimini
84010 Maiori (Salerno) / Via Casa Mannini, 10
Telephone: ++39 089 853547 / Fax: ++39 089 852048
E-Mail: info@casaraffaeleconforti.it / Web: www.casaraffaeleconforti.it

★★★ **Price Guide:** €43-€68 per person/day • Major Credit Cards accepted **Amenities:** Air conditioning • Bar • TV • Nearby airports are Naples • Nearest town is Salerno, Vietri Sul Mare, Minori, Amalfi and Positano • No Restaurant. Breakfast is included • Total number of rooms: 8 **Activities:** Beach, Boat Rental, Fishing, Shopping, ceramics **Additional Information:** 3rd and 4th bed €25 discount, children 0-10 years €30 • Half board/full board available.

This is quite an unusual type of accommodation for the Amalfi Coast. Casa Raffaele Conforti is located on the second floor of a 19th century noble mansion and is situated in the heart of the historical section of Maiori. The beach, being only one hundred meters away from the hotel, is ideal for family enjoyment.

The allure of ancient times is brought back to life through the frescos of the *Costaioli*, a typical style of painting in Maiori during the last century. The spaciousness of the bedrooms, each having its own bathroom and terrace, gives rise to comfortable quarters with the kids. The rooms have been furnished with antique furniture, but each is equipped with the modern comforts of air conditioning, telephone, TV, and radio. Casa Raffaele Conforti also has a bar, reading room, and private covered garage. Although there is no restaurant within the casa, breakfast is included. Half board enables your family to select from typical restaurants along the coast offering delightful meals. This is less restrictive when traveling with kids, giving you more flexibility where and when you eat.

Many excursions are available from this location. A company called Sunland organizes day trips to the top spots on the Amalfi coast. Their telephone number is 089 877 455, or fax at 089 877 781. The web is www.sunland.it. Either by sailing or a mini-cruise, visit hidden coves and towns from Maiori to Positano. Some of the finest ceramics available are in the town of Vietri Sul Mare, where generations of artisans skillfully design unique pieces of craftsmanship.

Grand Hotel Excelsior Vittoria

Owner/Managing Director: Dr. Luca Fiorentino
Piazza Torquato Tasso, 34 / 80067 Sorrento, Naples / Italy
Telephone: ++390818071044 / Fax: ++390818771206
E-Mail: reservations@exvitt.it / Web: www.exvitt.it

★★★★★ **Price guide:** €296-€2010/per room per night, chilren 4-12 years 50% discount • Major credit cards accepted **Amenities:** Air conditioning • Babysitting • 2 bars • Cable/Satellite TV • Internet access point • Laundry • Airports: Rome, Naples • Nearby towns: Sorrento, Rome and Amalfi Coast • Restaurants: 2; Breakfast included; lunch and dinner €38-€50; or à la carte • Total rooms: 105, including 15 suites & 3 apartments **Activities:** Boat rentals • Children's park • Dock: on the sea • Fishing • Massage: on request • Shopping: wooden marquetry, embroideries, music boxes and lace. • Swimming pool • Cultural tours **Additional Information:** Private lift/elevator to the harbor • Vittoria Restaurant: open all year • Bosquet Restaurant: panoramic view, open May to September • Both restaurants are open to guests and the general public • Private car parking • Special winter packages • Meeting facilities • Open all year • Half board/full board

The Grand Hotel Excelsior Vittoria is the ideal location to explore both the land and sea with children. A short 200-meter, private road lined with lemon, olive, and orange trees places you in Sorrento's charming main square. The shops are filled with skillfully created wooden marquetry, embroideries, and lace. We purchased a music box inlaid with the Star of David that plays, "I Will Return to Sorrento." My kids took pleasure in Go-Pedding through Sorrento's charmed streets filled with superb *gelaterias* and reached by easy access from the hotel. On the opposite side is an unsurpassable panorama encircling the Bay of Naples, Mount Vesuvius, and the favored islands of Capri and Ischia. An elevator transports you straight down to the sea and pier from the terrace. The concierge service can arrange cruises along this poetic coastline of Amalfi, Positano, and Ravello or inform you of the ferry schedule to the islands.

The day we ferried over the Isle of Capri, we encountered rough seas. The boys and I had an enjoyable ride on the outside boat deck. David, however, sat below in the enclosed area. As the waves heaved, so did the sightseers around him. By the time he reunited with us, he too, was ailing. Meandering through this enchanted island's streets and rocky beaches alleviated the discomfort he was feeling. We rode the cable car to the top of Capri where the view and pizza at Ristorante Pizzeria da Gemma, was comparably outstanding. David was admittedly apprehensive about embarking upon the ship for the

return trip, but he showed no sign of hesitation in following our lead to the outdoor level.

Throughout Italy, the mention of Sorrento is usually precipitated by an endorsement of the Grand Albergo Excelsior Vittoria. Seated near the terrace overlooking the sea, Dr. Luca Fiorentino and I spent innumerable hours conversing about his 160 year-old historic establishments. He is the forth generation of Fiorentinos to represent this gem. Preceding him was Raffaele, Onorato, and Ugo. He speaks enthusiastically about the re-emergence of family travel and has added a playground to commemorate this upsurge of young children sojourning here for the summer with their parents. Luca Fiorentino and his wife Lydia together have devoted themselves to this magnificently maintained grand villa that they want you to call your "home away from home." Dr. Fiorentino says, "People think of Florence as the cultural city of Italy, but Naples was one of the European capitals and is as equally important. We have here both the developed appreciation of the arts and natural beauty."

Sorrento was home to Alfredo and Pompeo Correale, know as the Counts of Terranova and the last descendants of this old Sorrentine family. Their wills made provisions for the estate that included the villa and art collections to be turned into Museo Correale di Terranovo. The inheritance also included the garden and farmland, which produces goods that are sold to benefit the operation of the museum. A few of Naples numerous sites of artistic and historic interest are Museo e Gallerie Capodimonte, Museo della Ceramica, Museo Archeologico Nazionale, Orto Botanico, in addition to an abundance of churches enriched with frescos and sculptures by famous Neapolitan artists. Expose your children to the once thriving civilizations of Cuma, Ercolano, Paesteum, and my kids' favorite, Pompeii. I am not sure what exactly intrigued them more - the gladiator barracks or the fresco on the wall next to the entrance to the "House of the Vetti of Priapus" weighing his gigantic phallus against a bag full of money on the other scale pan! It is worth the additional cost to hire a tour guide who will bring these ancient cities to life.

As Luca and I strolled through the rooms and corridors of his renowned hotel, he vividly recollected the days gone by. Each area and fresco has a story that brought further meaning to the present. Archeological pieces dating back to the 4th and 5th centuries C.E. tell us that a villa was located exactly where the Excelsior Vittoria stands today. During the restoration of 1982, original frescos painted in the 18th century by his great-grand uncle were found. The famous tenor, Enrico Caruso, occupied a suite in 1921 before he died in Naples. The Fiorentinos named this room after him, which boasts an extensive terrace that peers out to the port. Excelsior Vittoria has been a holiday home to many eminent people such as Emperors of Austria, Hungary, crown heads of Sweden, Wagner, Verdi, Alexandre Dumas, and Nietzsche. In more recent years, their guest list has included Luciano Pavarotti, Sophia Loren, Ronald Reagan, and Princess Margaret who also has a room bearing her namesake.

The hotel has 105 rooms including 15 suites. I favored the old-world charm of the Aurora Suite and the luxurious exclusive Pompeii suite decorated with frescos offering a breathtaking view of the Bay of Naples. The most majestic room of all is the Sala Vittoria dining room with a detailed 18th century fresco of cherubs, garlands, and wildflower bouquets. Your savory meals of *La Cucina Italiana* (the Italian kitchen) may be enjoyed here or on the open-air Bosquet Restaurant facing the Tyrrhenian Sea and Mount Vesuvius. Enticing snacks are available poolside amidst the immense park which encompasses it. A stay in Sorrento at the Excelsior Vittoria will not leave you guessing as to why it was included in the so-called "Grand Tour." This was a journey that every noble European son of the time was required to make in order for him to complete his cultural historical and worldly development.

❧ *Longing for Italy* ☙

DEBRA'S SENTIMENTS

Time and again when I am home in Atlanta, I crave the feeling of being in Italy. Since I cannot always fly off at a moment's notice, I do the next best thing. I make myself a cappuccino. Sipping this hot and sweet beverage transports me to a time and place—sitting at an outdoor café at the edge of Lake Como. My warm companion was tall, dark, and handsome with a brown rim around his white frothy collar. His name - cappuccino d' Italia. One smell, one drink, has captured me for eternity.

My appreciation for this drink has continued and grown since that first jet-lagged afternoon on Lago di Como's shore. That moment transformed my life forever. My pulse slowed down to match the tranquility and stillness of the water. Every emotion I was capable of feeling grew deeper as my awareness was heightened. I reached a place within myself that remained untouched after years of yoga and transcendental meditation. So when the mood strikes, I brew the cappuccino in my kitchen at home, open the latest edition of *La Cucina Italiana* magazine, the number one authority on Italian food and living, and start cooking.

Hotel Villa Maria & Hotel Giordano

Owner/Manager: Palumbo Family
Amalfi Coast / 84010 Ravello (Salerno) / Italy
Telephone: ++39089857170, 857319-857255-857071 / Fax +39-089857071
E-Mail: villamaria@villamaria / E-Mail: giordano@amalfinet.it / Web: www.villamaria.it

Hotel Villa Maria★★★★ and Hotel Giordano★★★ **Price Guide:** Villa Maria: €175-€215/Giordano€144-€170 • Major credit cards accepted **Amenities:** Air conditioning • Babysitting • Bar • Cable/Satellite TV • Internet: Villa Maria • Laundry • Airport: Naples • Nearby towns: Amalfi Coast and Naples • Restaurant: Breakfast included both hotels. Villa Maria's restaurant offers lunch & dinner à la carte • Total rooms: Villa Maria: 24 • Total rooms: Giordano: 31 **Activities:** Boat rentals • Children's park • Fishing • Gym • Horseback riding • Massage: upon request • Shopping: ceramics • Swimming pool: Hotel Giordano • Tennis Court: Hotel Giordano • Cultural tours, particularly walking tours **Additional Information:** Open all year • Culinary classes • Half board/full board

The intrigue of Ravello on the Amalfi Coast lies in its synthesis between nature and culture. Villa Maria is panoramically situated at the pinnacle of this charming, terraced, seaside resort. Park your cars in Ravello's main square, and follow the sign posts as you ascend the pathway up to Hotel Villa Maria and Hotel Giordano, where your family will receive a warm and friendly welcome from the Palumbo family.

The hotels are centrally located between the square and Villa Cimbrone. Although Hotel Villa Maria contains twenty-four well-appointed rooms, its overall size is petite. This creates an intimate, quiet atmosphere best suited for families with experienced young travelers. Our accommodations at Villa Maria were spacious and comfortable, with an expansive view of the Amalfi coast. As a guest of Villa Maria, you are welcome to make use of Hotel Giordano's pool.

Hotel Giordano shares the same ownership offering thirty-one comfortable rooms, an attractive swimming pool, and access to additional parking. Giordano is the best choice for families with children ten and younger. A closer proximity to the town center provides more activity and entertainment.

The secrets of the Amalfi Coast's ancient gastronomic culture are evident in their chef's discerning food preparation and taste. Whether dining *alfresco* with a captivating vista of the magnificent coast or inside their pleasant dining room with a garden view, you will behold the vision forever. Giving your kids an early appreciation of distinctly unusual food stimulates their mind, opening their eyes to the vastness of the world.

Ravello is an enchanting village with many sights to explore with kids. We were happiest enjoying the splendor of the sea, intermingled with a bit of cultural appreciation. The ceramics of Amalfi are some of the finest we have discovered in Italy. Many artists and writers have been drawn here for inspiration in their diverse and remarkable works; furthermore, Ravello has been the backdrop to numerous films, while Gore Vidal calls it "the most beautiful in the world."

Romantik Hotel & Restuarant Villa Cheta Elite

Owner/Manager: Stefania Aquadro
85041 Aquafredda Maratea (Potenza) / Italy
Telephone: ++39 0973 878 134 / Fax: ++39 0973 878 135
E-Mail: villacheta@tin.it or info@villacheta.it / Web: www.villacheta.it

★★★★ **Price Guide:** €72-€119 for double occupancy, children 0-10 years 50% discount in room with parents • Major Credit Cards accepted **Amenities:** Air conditioning • Bar • TV • Laundry • Nearby airport: Naples • Nearest town: Maratia, Aquafreda and Mt. S.Biagio • Breakfast and dinner is included. • Total number of rooms - 18 **Activities:** Private Beach • Boat Rental • Fishing • Shopping, straw baskets, copper and raw iron • Tennis court, 1km • Cultural, historic and natural tours of Parco del Pollino **Additional Information:** Yoga courses offered

Disembarking the ferry from Messina, Sicily to Reggio di Calabria, the boot tip of Italy, we drove up the southwestern coast of Maratea. There are breathtaking coastal views with high mountains, whose abrupt pointed peaks appear to rise endlessly while overlooking blue-green, colored waters. Maratea is a tranquil seaside resort encapsulated by luxuriant vegetation. At Villa Cheta Elite, you will experience this unspoiled natural setting in the Aquadro family's charming villa.

The Marsicano family built this 18th century liberty type villa. Donna Marsicano was a passionate cook who created delicious dishes with select wines of the region for other noble families. In 1982, Villa Cheta Elite was transformed into a hotel but has maintained much of the original tradition. Still present are the art nouveau era glass panels and lamps. Throughout the villa, their family's antique furniture gives each room an individual feel.

The lace napkins and tablecloths reflect the outstanding quality of their restaurant and service.

The emphasis is on traditional regional cooking and their specialty is fish. The climate was mild affording us the opportunity to be served breakfast and dinner on the terraces where fleeting views of the Gulf of Policastro can be seen through the bougainvillea and rich landscape. The same staff at Villa Cheta have been dedicated to the refined service during its twenty years of operation. Biaggio, the maître d'hôtel, has a constant eye out for that which you may desire.

The beach can be reached by a walkway cascading from the hotel to the sea. Kayaks and paddleboats are available to rent. An outdoor café serves light fare and refreshments. Venturing out further from the hotel you will discover other beaches and the Aqua Parco (water park) located on the shore of Praia a Mare. The boys enjoyed several hours of rides and amusements while David and I swam and sunbathed in the adjacent sea.

Stefania and her husband, Peter, invite you and your kids to stay at Villa Cheta Elite while enjoying the same gracious hospitality begun centuries ago.

Il Melograno

Owner: Guerra Family / General Manager: Camillo Guerra / Director: Roberta Guerra
70043 Monopoli (Bari) / Contrada Torricella 345 / I-70043 Monopoli - Bari / Italy
Telephone: ++39 080 6909030 / Fax: ++39 080 747908
E-Mail: melograno@melograno.com / Web: www.melograno.com

★★★★★ **Price Guide:** €280–€760/daily per person, children 2-6 years €90/over 6 years €120 with extra bed in parents room • Major Credit Cards accepted **Amenities:** Air conditioning • Babysitting • Bar • TV • Internet • Laundry • Nearby airports are Bari, Brindisi • Nearest town is Monopoli, Alberobello, Polignano, Ostuni, and Grottaglie. • Two restaurants. Breakfast is included. • Total number of rooms: 38 with 8 suites **Activities:** Biking • Boat Rental • Fishing • Golf, 10km • Walking • Horseback riding, 6km • Massage on request • Private beach, 7km • Shopping in Monopoli, specialty items are terra cotta whistles • Three salt water swimming pools • Tennis court • Tours of cultural sites, and tours of caves **Additional Information:** Half board/full board available. • Ala Cart menu is offered • Cooking classes and instruction in homemade orecchiette (short pasta) and mozzarella. Classes offered twice a year; first two weeks of April and first week of November.

When Franco Ottaviani, the General Manager of La Posta Vecchia, e-mailed me to recommend Il Melograno, I knew it must be an exceptional destination. In a lesser-known corner of Italy, once part of Magna Grecia, this 16th century farmhouse was originally built as protection against Saracen and Byzantine invaders. In 1970, the Guerra family purchased this *masseria* (fortified farmhouse) as a summer home. By 1986, restoration had begun in an effort to transform it to the luxurious Five-Star hotel it is today.

Camillo Guerra, an art and antique dealer, has personally furnished each room, retaining the warmth and hospitality of her family's retreatful abode. The rooms are elegantly situated around the main piazza, where in the evening we appreciated the music of a talented violinist. Il Melograno is set on an exquisite estate surrounded by olive, prickly pear, almond, and citrus trees, which provide the oil, fresh juice, and marmalades they serve to you each day.

Il Ristorante Melograno specializes in the highly praised *Pugliese* (Puglia region) version of Mediterranean cuisine. The hotel garden seasonally provides many of the vegetables used to create the delectable dishes we couldn't resist over-indulging in during our stay. Typically in the finer restaurants throughout Italy, each course is a sufficient amount to appreciate the taste, but at Il Melgrano, any one part of the meal is sufficient as the entire dinner. Embarrassingly, by the third plateful, we were all pushing our food around, hoping to give the impression that we ate. After a short walk, however, we managed to devour Il Melgrano's irresistible desserts.

Il Melgrano is positioned between Bari and Brindisi, lending itself to many daily excursions. The caves of Castellana and Trulli style architecture of Alberobello, both recognized as universal treasures, are a short ride away. Fascinating medieval towns, particularly Polignano, zoo, golf, and horseback riding are nearby. An ideal family excursion is an afternoon fishing on Il Melgrano's boat, which includes your personal captain with meals provided.

The main villa has a pool, while La Peschiera is a private beach facility with two additional swimming pools, bar, and extraordinary seafood restaurant. It was built on the foundation of an ancient fishery. Located 8 kilometers from Il Melgrano, it is only open during the summer months.

The Melograno, or pomegranate with its large brilliant red flowers and fruit, is said to "…immortalize the one that tastes them while loving and believing in love." A stay at Il Melograno is to be raptured in the illusion of eternity. It is no wonder that Mel Gibson was here prior to our stay, vacationing with his family and considering this as his future movie site.

Tenuta del Barco

Relais di Campagna sul Mare alla / Masseria Porvica / Owner/Manager: Maria Cristina & Nick Donadio
74026 Marina di Pulsano (Taranto) / Puglia, Italy
Telephone/Fax: ++39 099 5333051/++39059921323
E-Mail: tenuta@iname.com / Web: www.tenutadelbarco.com

★★★★ **Price Guide:** Cottages from €499-€1149; Apartments from €619=€1749 per week • All Major Credit Cards accepted **Amenities:** Agrituristica • Air conditioning in cottages only • Laundry • Nearby airports are Brindisi • Nearest town is Taranto and Pulsano • Restaurant. • Total number of rooms: 17, cottages: 10, and apartments: 7
Activities: Biking • Boat Rental • Bocce • Children's Park • Horseback riding • Jogging • Semi-private beach • Soccer field • Tennis court • Waterpark, Acqua Folies **Additional Information:** Restaurant serves fresh produce and wine from Agroturismo's land

For a vacation away from the daily pressures of life, look no further. Tenuta del Barco has it all; however, when owner Nick Donadio described his family's 250-year-old vast and remote 100-hectare (0.40 = 1 acre) farming estate, I had no idea it would take a *Carabinari* (police) escort to help us find it. Upon our arrival, the office manager, Marisa Petzella, was there to receive our family. The boys were hungry and quick to inquire about food. Although we were too late for lunch and too early for dinner, Marisa changed her hat, stepped into the kitchen, and arranged plates of Tenuta del Barco's fruits, vegetables, cheese, bread, olive oil, and wine. We dined on their patio, relaxed and content as though we had spent the morning personally harvesting the crops. The hospitality continued throughout our stay. On July 4th, Nick surprised us with an "Independence Day" celebration. A festive evening meal was accompanied by an accordion player singing a repertoire of classic American songs, which of course included "New York, New York."

The Barco estate has been restored in authentic Mediterranean style. The residences have a rustic decor featuring vaulted ceilings made of Carparino slate. Each apartment has one or two rooms, and all are equipped with a kitchenette and facilities with accommodations for the handicapped. The guestrooms also face the courtyard. The recently constructed cottages are more modernized and include air conditioning.

The Tenuta highlights a tennis court, soccer field, *bocce* ball bowling green, and a jogging course. Bicycles can be rented for excursions to the sea by way of the old sheep tracks. As guests of Tenuta del Barco, your family has use of a full-service beach, which also rents kayaks and pedal boats. Horseback riding is nearby along with Acqua Folies, a fun water park that Ari and Isaac thoroughly enjoyed. They also recommend the park's brick oven pizza.

The stillness of the evening at Tenuta del Barco lends itself to cohesive family time — drive a few kilometers to Pulsano for la Gelateri di Pulsano's extraordinary array of *gelato* (ice cream), then relax in Tenuta's peaceful courtyard with a book or play family games. We used our laptop one evening to watch movies we had brought from home. I admit it was quite *Americana* of us, nevertheless entertaining.

Eremo Della Giubiliana

Owner: Salvatore Mancini Nifosi / Director: Anastasia Gurrieri
Contrada Giubiliana / 97100 Ragusa (Ragusa) / Italy
Telephone: ++39 0932 669119/669129 / Fax: ++39 0932 669129
E-Mail: info@eremodellaguibiliana.it / Web: www.eremodellaguibiliana.it

★★★★★ **Price Guide:** €120–€450 per person/day, children 0-2 years free/2-4 years 50% discount/4-8 years 30% discount • Major Credit Cards accepted **Amenities:** Five stars • Air conditioning • Babysitting • Bar • Internet • Laundry • Nearby airport is Catania • Nearest town is Ragusa. • Two Restaurants. Breakfast is included. • Total number of rooms is 9 **Activities:** Biking • Boating • Fishing • Hiking • Massage • Private Beach, 9km • Shopping • Swimming pool • Cultural, historic, and scenic tours • Water park called Castellana Park **Additional Information:** Half board/full board available.

Board your private aircraft and fly directly from any European country to Eremo della Giubiliana's airfield, open exclusively to tourist traffic and general aviation aircraft. Upon landing, you will immediately recognize that the ability to fly to this five-star hotel on Sicily, in the middle of the Mediterranean, is only one of Eremo della Giubiliana's outstanding features.

The history is as remarkable as the accompanying amenity list. The estate was once a part of the old Ecclesiastical Fife of Renna in the 12th century. As a former Arabic-fortified structure, its position over the course of history afforded protection from the frequent raids of the Barbary pirates since the end of the 15th century when they acted as privateers for the Turkish Empire. In the first half of the 16th century, the Knights of the Order of St. John, on the way to the Isle of Malta, occupied the convent. In the 18th century, the Hermitage was bought by the Nifosi's, a family of the land aristocracy of the Hyblean Highlands. In 1997, Vincenza Jolanda Nifosi began restoration, transforming the estate to its original purpose of providing a hospitable sanctuary for his guests. Eremo della Giubiliana lies on the southeastern part of Sicily in Contrada Giubiliana. Ragusa is the nearest town, just ten kilometers from the hotel; however, we were happy to relax by the swimming pool, and eat lunch in the private garden of the Nifosi family. The feeling was that of an intimate oasis — who needed to go anywhere else?

We have visited hotels in nearly every region of Italy, and up to this time, no other facility offers such vast and unusual services. The Dragut, a 28-foot cabin cruiser, offers daily excursions along the Sicilian coast or two-day trips to the island of Malta. The boat is able to accommodate up to six people and is equipped for snorkeling, game fishing, and scuba diving. Book your flight on Eremo della Giubiliana's private plane at reception one day in advance, choosing from eight scenic tours: the south-east coast; the Baroque towns and Noto; cave and mountain tour; Swabian castles tour; Grand Tour of Etna; the central part of Sicily, Enna and the Tower of Frederico II; the Aeolian islands; and the Agrigento temples tour.

Should you choose to keep your feet on solid ground, Eremo della Guibiliana has a guidebook illustrating trekking routes from the hotel through ancient and medieval paths. A short distance from the hotel you will discover the beach town of Marina di Ragusa. Ari and Isaac had the best time climbing on the jetties while searching for and catching crabs.

Eremo della Giubiliana's cuisine is inspired by the typical highland aristocratic recipes. The main ingredients are organic products from the farm and various types of cheeses. Each day they prepare hand-made pasta, breads, and *Focacce* (thick pizza bread without cheese) from their own wheat flower. The choices always vary offering two separate menus: *La Masseria Del Mare* (the fish menu), and *La Masseria Di Terra* (the meat menu). You are welcome to choose different courses from each. For antipaste, don't miss *formaggio arrosto al miele degli iblei* (roasted Ragusano cheese dressed with honey). On our second night, we dined *al fresco* (outdoors) with a family from Los Angeles, the Rosenthal's and their two daughters. Having ordered different menu selections, we couldn't resist tasting from each other's plates. The Sicilian wines, especially the Corleone, delicately complimented the meal. Do save room for their typical Sicilian desserts of Ricotta cheese, fruits, and chocolate.

Our time spent at Eremo della Giubiliana was enhanced by the continual attention of Anastasia Gurrieri, the Director. Salvatore Mancini Nifosi, the heir to this noble land, has a continual yet unobtrusive demeanor. His passion for Eremo della Giubiliana is expressed throughout the estate. As a renowned architect, his skillful eye is reflected in the constant renovation and extensions to his property. The latest additions to the nine Sicilian-style hotel rooms are the cottages directly on the airfield offering both nightly and weekly rates. The thick walls of the Hermitage and vast wilderness of this area lend itself to a peaceful stay. A visit to Eremo della Giubiliana is an opportunity to discover Sicily and its African boundary.

Hotel Carasco

Owner/Manager: Hermione & Marco Del Bono
Porto dell Genti 98055 / 98055 Lipari / Isola di- Eolie-Sicily / Italy
Telephone: ++39 090 9811605 / Fax: ++39 090 9811828
E-Mail: carasco@tin.it / Web: www.carasco.it

★★★ **Price Guide:** €55-€150 per person • Major Credit Cards accepted **Amenities:** Air conditioning • Bar • TV • Internet • Nearby airports are Naples, Palermo, Catania, Reggio Calabria • By ship: Milazzo • By hydrofoil: Milazzo, Messina, Reggio Calabria, Naples, and Palermo • Restaurant. Breakfast is included. • Total number of rooms: 89 **Activities:** Biking • Boating • Fishing • Beach • Rock Terrace • Sauna • Sailing • Water skiing • Scuba Diving • Snorkeling • Wind surfing • Shopping for high fashion, island apparel, jewelry • Sea water swimming pool with Jacuzzi • Cultural tours and other Eolian islands **Additional Information:** Piano bar • Conference facility • Half board/full board available. • Discounts: 10% 1 week stay, Additional adult bed 30%, Seniors 10%, Honeymooners 10%, children 0-4 70%, 5-14 50% when staying with parents and up to 14 in a separate room 20%, all exclude August

Hotel Carasco is the manifestation of Marco Del Bono's dreams. He designed the hotel and, together with his wife Hermione, runs it with the eyes of parents watching over their children. The panoramic vistas will capture you from any angle you gaze. The hotel appears to emerge from the azure sea below, maintaining continuity with its surroundings of pastel, multi-colored vegetation. Their restaurant, serving local and Sicilian specialties, has far-reaching views of Lipari and the sea below.

Hotel Carasco holds the keystone position on one of the most beautiful bays on the Island of Lipari. A short, one-kilometer walk or the hotel's shuttle bus quickly places you in the heart of Marina Corta, the favored *piazza* (town square) of the island, alongside the local harbor. The kids absolutely relished their time here at Hotel Carasco. The sea water swimming pool, the children's area and Jacuzzi, a cascading rock terrace beneath with private access to the sea, fishing, snorkeling, scuba diving, and boating excursions were just some of the highlights.

To celebrate my 46th birthday, Hermione arranged for us to be picked up by a private boat below the hotel. We spent the day exploring the surrounding islands and swimming in secluded blue grottoes and off remote beaches. The boys had fun jumping and diving from the cliffs. The pleasures of the day were enhanced by our meal at "Trattoria da Pina" on the island of Vulcano. Typical Sicilian cuisine of Aeolian fresh fish and vegetables were served. Our driver called ahead for reservations at 090-9852-242, due to its limited seating capacity.

The Del Bonos are present throughout the day to suggest and organize day trips on Lipari or to the other Aeolian islands. They particularly recommend a boat trip to the island of Panarea to swim in the bay of "Cala Junca" and a visit to the prehistoric village. No matter what you choose to do, an unforgettable holiday awaits you at this ideal family resort, with a child friendly attitude and access to loads of fun activities.

Hotel Relais Modica

Owner/Manager: Antonio Modica & Francesca Baccolini
Via Tommasco Campailla N 99 / 97015 Modica (Ragusa) / Italy
Telephone: ++39 0932 754 451 / Fax: ++39 0932 754 451
Cell: ++39 339 2048498 / Cell: ++39 339 31 23957
E-Mail: hotelrelaismodica@virgilio.it / Web: www.paginegialle.it\hotelrelaismodica

★★ **Price Guide:** €75–€88 for a double • Major Credit Cards accepted are Visa, MasterCard, and Maestro **Amenities:** Air conditioning • Babysitting • Bar • TV • Internet • Nearby airport is Catania Airport • Nearest town is Modica, and Ragusa • No Restaurant. Breakfast is included. • Total number of rooms: 10 **Activities:** Beach, 15km • Boat Rental, 15km • Shopping: specialty items embroidery and chocolate **Additional Information:** Typical Sicilian restaurants within walking distance. In room delivery service from most area restaurants.

Upon leaving Ragusa, Anastasia, the manager of Eremo della Giubiliana directed us to the town of Modica. There we would find Antica Dolceria Bonajuto (www.bonajuto.it), an old fashion pastry and sweet shop. Since 1880, the art and story of chocolate takes you back in history when Sicily, and particularly Modica, were united with Spain and found their roots in the ceremonial civilization of Meso-America and the Aztecs. The Spanish found *xocoátl*, a product made from cocoa seeds and held in high regard, for it represented strength, vigor, and wealth. Today, using the same techniques as his great-grandfather, Francor Ruta and his wife, Nicotra Grazia, with their son, Pierpaola Ruta, masterfully recreate exquisite cakes of Arabian and Spanish origin, along with some of the most unusual and sensuous flavors of chocolate. My most memorable was *cioccolatini al peperoncino confezione* (chocolate with chili peppers). The movie *Chocolat* is recaptured in this *dolceria* (sweet shop). The family is eager to show you their procedures and perhaps share a taste of their masterful food.

The baroque town of Modica is a gem for those who are able to appreciate a life unspoiled by modern tourist attractions. So taken by the antiquity and perhaps the chocolate, we postponed a night in Taormina.

To reach Hotel Relais Modica, you ascend numerous steps winding up to an ancient gate. Here you will be welcomed by Antonio, Francesca and their two young daughters, Sophia and Agnese. They have done an extraordinary job modernizing this ten-bedroom hotel. A bed and breakfast by design, but should you desire additional meals at the Relais Modica, they will arrange anything you want from the local Sicilian restaurants. Personally, we enjoyed the best pizza we had in the entire region at La Contea Pizzeria on the ancient Via Grimaldi. Choose from forty-two different types of pizza to include *pizza dessert* with *nutella* and *panna* (chocolate and cream) or chips (French fries). The boys each started out with an order of French fries, freshly made, hot and plentiful. They have adapted the Italian way of eating them with ketchup and mayonnaise. The local table wine was light and refreshing. After dinner we strolled the streets of Modica, discovering Café Del Arte serving *I Dolci Della Tradizione Modicana* (traditional desserts and sweets of Modica) and famous for their chocolate *gelato* (ice cream) with chili peppers. After the kids went to bed, Antonio, Francesca, David, and I sat outside on the roof garden relaxing with a cold glass of *lemoncello* (lemon liquor). The city below was completely illuminated with small white lights outlining the city's many prominent structures. Antonio proudly identified the Duomo di F. Giorgio, La Chiesa Madre di F. Pietro, and important castles of the city.

For an authentic perspective of Sicilian culture, hospitality, and some of the most outstanding white sandy beaches with azure blue waters, a visit to Hotel Relais Modica is not only unforgettable, it's mandatory!

Hotel Villa Belvedere

Owner/Manager: Christian Pecaut
79 Via Bagnoli Croce, / 79-98039 Taormina (ME) / Italy
Telephone: ++39 0942 23791 / Fax: ++39 0942 625830
E-Mail: info@villabelvedere.it / Web: www.villabelvedere.it

★★★ **Price Guide:** €110–€190/double, €150–€250/triple • Credit Cards accepted are Visa, MasterCard and EuroCard **Amenities:** Air conditioning • Bar • TV • Internet • Nearby airports are Catania • Nearest town is Taormina. • Restaurant. Breakfast included. Lunch served 11 to 4 • Total number of rooms: 50, & 2 suites **Activities:** Children's Park • Shopping, high fashion, pottery, leather, jewelry, wine and antiques • Swimming pool • Cultural tours of other cities, archeological and Mt. Etna • Golf course at foot of Mt. Etna, near Linguaglossa (30 minutes) **Additional Information:** Closed November 25th through April 30th

Taormina is famous not only for its mild climate, which is usually spring-like, but especially for its beautiful panoramas, ancient monuments, and wide variety of Sicilian and Italian products found along its unique traffic-free *corso* (road). Its popularity has grown stronger through the years due in part to its chic allure, contemporary nightlife, and entertainment. Every summer, from the middle of July through the first week of September, Taormina is host to an international festival called Taormina Arte. This event combines a world film festival, many concerts, operas, and plays, all taking place in the 3rd century B.C.E. Greek Theater. Taormina also has several discos and nightclubs.

With all this enticement, the hotels are generally full to capacity and the need to encourage family travel to their destination is not necessary. I telephoned nearly fifteen resort owners and managers, each kind and cordial, but not eager to promote kids in their hotel. Christian Pecaut feels different about his family-run hotel. He is the great-grandson of the founder of Villa Belvedere, built in 1902, which is one of the oldest hotels in Taormina. He, too, was fully booked yet managed to create accommodations in a cottage on the property.

A continual revamping to modernize the grounds and facility has not detracted from Villa Belvedere's original warm and friendly atmosphere. The most outstanding feature is the swimming pool area surrounded by luxurious tropical gardens, cascading towards the Mediterranean Sea. From most of Villa Belvedere's rooms and terraces, you can appreciate views of the shoreline and Mt. Etna in the distance. The hotel has a terraced restaurant alongside the pool where lunch and refreshments are served every day from 11:00 a.m. to 4:00 p.m. Mr. Pecaut and his staff will guide you to special restaurants for dinner or just stroll through Taormina, stopping for a glass of wine, pizza, and gelato along the way.

Hotel Villa Belvedere is ideally located adjacent to Taormina's public gardens where there is a recreation area for children, which tends to act as a shelter from the hastened life of the town center; nevertheless, Villa Belvedere is only five minutes away from many of the historical sites, cable car, and stone steps leading to the sea. The personal service guaranteed by the Pecaut family ensures that your family will leave Villa Belvedere with the peacefulness of a restful holiday.

Villa Meligunis Hotel

Owner/Manager: Giusina & Manuela Tiraboschi d'Ambra
Via Marte 7 / 98055 Lipari / Isole Eolie (Messina) / Italy
Telephone: ++39 090 9812426 / Fax: ++39090 9880149
E-Mail: mailto:villameligunis@netnet.it / Web: www.villameligunis.it

★★★★ **Price Guide:** Hotel: €120–€290 per person per night, Agave Residence: €150–€200 per person per night • Major Credit Cards accepted **Amenities:** Air conditioning • Babysitting • Bar • TV • Internet • Laundry • Nearby airports are Naples, Palermo, Catania and Reggio Calabria • Nearest towns are Lipari, Milazzo, and Naples by ship, Milazzo, Messina, Reggio Calabria, Naples and Palermo by hydrofoil. • Restaurant. Breakfast is included. • Total number of rooms: 32 **Activities:** Beach – free shuttle • Biking • Boat Rental • Conference facilities • Fishing • Scuba diving • Snorkeling • Water skiing • Sailing and wind surfing • Shopping, high fashion and island apparel • Food and jewelry • Cultural tours of volcanos and other eolian islands. **Additional Information:** Half board/full board available. Discounts available: additional bed 20%, children infant-10 - 50%, 11-14 - 30%

A s we disembarked the passenger ferry from Naples onto the Aeolian island of Lipari, we were kindly greeted port-side by the staff of Villa Meliguinis. Delayed three hours, hungry, and overtired from a journey which had begun in the United States nearly two days before, we were finally here! Manuela, the owner and manager of this illustrious hotel, thoughtfully had their Chef Maurizio arrange antipasti, breads, and drinks along with an inaugural bottle of Aeolian red wine. Indeed, a warm family-friendly welcome!

Too excited to sleep after our long voyage, David and I set out to discover the ancient center of Lipari. Just outside our door was the old and serene fisherman's quarter of Marina Corta. At this late hour of 12:00 a.m., the town was full of life. The labyrinth mazes of small streets were lined with island shops of high fashion and jewelry, along with trattorias and cafés. For years we have been coming to Italy in search of a tropical island encompassing both beauty and the ethnicity of Italian culture, so evident here on Lipari

Our accommodations in the new four star annex, "Agave Residence," of Villa Meliguinis was ideal. Manuela affectionately refers to the six skillfully renovated apartments as "her baby," offering families the privacy of their own home as they are equipped with a modern kitchenette, full bath, telephone, and air conditioning, while providing all the services available at Hotel Villa Meliguinis. The main hotel is in an historic villa of the 18th century with thirty-two rooms offering discrete luxury and comfort. All the rooms have their own bathrooms, air conditioning, mini bar, satellite television, telephone, balcony, or terrace, most with panoramic views. A breakfast buffet and table service offering hot drinks awaits you each morning.

The expert staff of Villa Meliguinis can arrange excursions on any of the Aeolian Islands: Lipari, the largest island, has a recreation of a Bronze Age Acropolis; six churches in various architectural styles from Norman to 18th century Baroque; an archeological museum housing 4,000 years of history; the pumice-stone quarries of Canneto and Campo Bianco and some of the finest panoramas. Salina is known to be the greenest of the islands and is composed of six extinct volcanos. Caper bushes and vines grow on its terraced hillsides. Stromboli, with its eruptive volcano, is the most spectacular to view. To get there, take either a three-hour rugged climb by foot, or observe from a boat the infamous flow of smoking and luminescent lava along its crevasse. The volcano, a 21 kilometer island is actually composed of four volcanos. According to mythology, this is where

Vulcan, the "God of Fire," made his advances, hence the expression "Vulcanism."

Villa Meliguinis also offers shuttle service to and from the beach of Canneto where the hotel provides umbrellas and sun chairs while taking personal care of you. They can also organize nighttime fishing excursions with dinner on a traditional Aeolian boat. A swimming pool is being constructed for the 2003 season, accurately upgrading this hotel to a five star experience.

I saved the best for last! The terrace of Villa Meliguinis contains an outstanding restaurant Le Terrazze matched only by its panoramic view and elegant service. It's only open only during the summer months, serving exquisite Aeolian dishes. So much of what Villa Meliguinis stands for is expressed through their cuisine - imaginative, sophisticated, and rich. Chef Maurizio is at your disposal for any special request you might have, but his daily ever-changing menu features items such as *ravioli di pesce all' isolana* (ravioli stuffed with fish and dressed with light fish sauce), *filetto ai funghi* (filet of beef with mushrooms), *pomodorini rucola e capper* (cherry tomatoes, rucola, with their superb fresh island capers),and the *tartufo al cioccolato affogato al caffé* (chocolate truffle with hot coffee poured over it) should only leave you yearning *per l'amore* for your sweetheart.

Manuela, her mother Giusina, and their staff are looking forward to welcoming your family to their island to share the wealth of history, sea, and island pleasures.

Costa Smeralda / The Luxury Collection
Starwood Hotels & Resorts
Area Manager Costa Smeralda: Marco Milocco
Area Director of Sales & Marketing: Jan Pachner / General Manager Hotel Romazzino: Milton Sgarbi
07020 Porto Cervo / Sardinia, Italy
Telephone: ++ 39 0789977111 / Fax: ++ 39 0789977618
E-mail: res067romazzino@starwood.com / Website: www.luxurycollection.com/romazzino

★★★★★ **Price Guide:** €500–€1320/per person/per day/Half Board • *Presidential Suite* with its own gym • price on request • Major credit cards accepted • Opened: April-October • Nearest airport: Costa Smeralda Airport in Olbia • Nearest harbors: Olbia and Golfo Aranci • Nearest towns: Olbia, Porto Cervo, and Porto Rotondo **Amenities:** 94 luxuriously appointed guest rooms, including 78 double rooms, 4 one-bedroom suites, 10 open plan suites, and one Presidential and one Royal, all with private terrace featuring either sea views or garden views • Restaurants: *The Barbeque/* beach side • *The Romazzino/* panoramic sea view serving breakfast, lunch and dinner • Bars: Pool side and the *Ginepro Bar/* panoramic terrace • Italian designer boutique shops **Activities/Services:** Pool • Private Beach • Water Skiing • Tennis • Fitness Center/Personal Trainer available • Cycling • Table Tennis • Mini-soccer Field • Baby-sitting/on request • Business Center • All day entertainment for kids • Boutiques • Car rental • Car parking area • Multilingual Concierge and reception desk staff • Cribs and high chairs • Currency exchange • Doctor on request • Safe deposit boxes in rooms and at reception • Horseback riding (20 minutes) • Pevero Golf Course (5 minutes) • Porter Service • Laundry and Pressing/ same day service • Nurse on request • Luggage storage room • Massages • 24 Hour Room Service • Hairdresser and Beauty Salon • Flowers/on request • Fax and Cable • Photocopies • Newspaper delivered daily • Boat rental (Marinsarda) • Go Carting (20 Minutes) • Kayaking • Mountain Biking • Fishing • Sailing • Snorkeling • Scuba Diving • Wind Surfing **Additional Information:** In addition to the extensive range of sports and services, the following excursions and activities may be organized: ride on a characteristic steam engine • visit to the grottos of Ispinigoli, and Blue Marino • excursion to the Archaeological site of Li Muri • explore typical little villages and landscapes of Gallura (region of Sardinia) • boat to nearby islands of Motorio, Soffi, or Maddalena • boat to the *Bocche di Bonifacio* of Corsica and play golf at the Sperone Golf Course • demonstrations of Sardinian handicrafts of tapestries, jewelry, and wood carving • shopping in Porto Cervo and Porto Rotondo • or visit the famous Cerasarda pottery factory • Starwood Hotels and Resorts are developing the same kid's project in other places on the Costa Smeralda, such as their *Hotel Cala di Volpe* and restaurant *Pomodoro*

The Hotel Romazzino sits on the most romantic coastal region of this Mediterranean Island of Sardinia. This famous area with outstanding scenery, turquoise sea, fantastic rock structures, complemented by the continual aroma of rosemary and thyme, is known as the Costa Smeralda, or emerald coastline. For forty years, well-off international clientele who can opt for anything in the world have retreated to this paradise and the unsurpassed pampering of Hotel Romazzino. In 1965, the famous Italian architect, Michele Busiri Vici, designed this dazzling white Moorish-style structure, which stands in utter contrast to the green landscape and deep blue of the sea and sky. Winding down through paths lined with flowering gardens and illimitable herbs is a grand elliptical shaped swimming pool and the longest hotel beach on Sardinia. Then there is the food… *The Barbeque* restaurant features an extensive antipasti buffet. Close at hand is a California, open-style kitchen, preparing freshly caught fish, sushi, meat, and pasta. In addition, there is a brick oven where the chef's

will bake pizza to suit your personal yearning. Then, their professional and friendly wait staff serves your food. As the sun sets, the terrace of The Romanzzino Restaurant affords not only breathtaking views but also the opportunity to taste more of their outstanding Mediterranean cuisine. Incidentally, should you desire something that's not on the menu, their obliging staff will respond to your request by saying, "It's my pleasure sir or madam" then, as if they had already anticipated your order, it appears. However, the best part of all this, is that the Romazzino is a family hotel.

Mr. Sgarbi, the general manager, is excited about their new *Toy Club Romazzino* for children. This *Kid's Club* concept is the first of its kind developed for luxury hotels. Here, children have personalized treatment, the same level of quality as adults. At the *Toy Club* playing is important business. Therefore, everything has been thought of to guarantee that the adults will not interrupt the children's world and vice versa. They have a dedicated staff of caregivers and entertainers, in addition to designated areas for kids to play and have fun all day. The activities consist of organized games, crafts, and sports. Admission is open to kids from three to twelve years of age. The *Toy Club* begins at ten in the morning continuing throughout the day until half past ten in the evening. Nonetheless, lunch is family time with parents at *The Barbecue* by the beach, whereas they suggest dinner with all the other children at the main restaurant.

As aforementioned in the amenities description, at hand is an endless array of continual activities. For children thirteen and over, and those younger with an independent nature, they will never be at a loss for something to do. My kids enjoyed the unlimited availability of all the water sports. David and I appreciated relaxing time together, knowing that the children were in a safe environment with attentive staff. From time to time, we joined them for various activities. Most memorable for myself was the morning we all went water-skiing. The instruction was supreme, as was the excitement of skiing concurrently, side-by-side, with Jacob, Isaac, and another boy they befriended named Alex. David devised a mini Olympics inclusive of an informal soccer game. We always joined together to take pleasure in the lavishly delicious cuisine.

It's no wonder why families return time and again to Hotel Romazzino, for the best of everything and anything you could wish for, awaits you at this magnificent five star luxury resort.

Twilight dinner at Club Hotel Li Capanni, Cannigione (Sardinia)

Hotel Villa Las Tronas

Owner/Manager: Dr.Vito La Spina
Lungomare Valencia, 1 / 07041 Alghero, Italy
Telephone: ++39 079 981818 / Fax: ++39 079 981044
E-mail: info@hvlt.com / Website: www.hvlt.com

★★★★ **Price Guide:** €180–€430 • Major credit cards accepted • Nearest airport: Alghero • Nearest Harbor: Alghero • Nearest town: Alghero **Amenities:** Situated on a private promontory on the shore of Alghero • 20 rooms some offering terraces, sea or park views, 2 junior suites, 3 deluxe suites • Air-conditioning • Telephone • Television • Mini-bar • Security box • Free parking • Park, piers, and terraces over the sea • Conference room • Small pet allowed • Open all year • Restaurant: Contemporary Mediterranean Cuisine, serving breakfast, lunch and dinner • Half board/Full board available **Activities:** Gym • Mountain bikes • Sea water swimming pool • Private rocky coast-line with safe swimming all around the hotel property **Additional Information:** 20% discount on the rate of half or full board for children under 12 years of age

Villa Las Tronas was built in 1880. Until the 1940's, it remained as the residence of Italian Royalty during their holidays in Sardinia. Renovated in 2000, Villa Las Tronas maintains its original historic atmosphere of a noble retreat. The Villa is located on a small private cape at the outskirts of Alghero. The hotel is surrounded by a park which is completely encompassed by a controlled access gate, separating this exclusive oasis from the town traffic, which assures guests a relaxing stay.

The swimming pool sits terraced above the

sea, surrounded below by outcroppings of rocky jetties. An additional terrace is to be found below adjoining the shores, with steps leading directly into the sea. Refreshments are served at these locations, making for a restful day.

The restaurant at Villa Las Tronas served the freshest of food amid impeccable taste and style. The menu changed each day, offering various gourmet preparations of vegetables, fish, and meats. The local Sardinian wines, produced with the *Vermentino* grapes, were a delicious accompaniment to our meals together with a captivating view of a gulf that has been defined as one of the most beautiful of the Mediterranean Sea.

Alghero was founded by the Doria in 1102 and then conquered by the Aragonese-Catalans in 1353. By 1541, many significant events had occurred, leaving the crown in the hands of Spanish rulers. Even today, the local people still call the town *Barcelloneta*, little Barcellona. A pleasant way to view the town is by bike, which Villa Las Tronas will supply. The ride along the sea towards the old part of town is best. The kid's took a short walk from the hotel to the aquarium, which they described as, "a small but fascinating collection of exotic fish."

Alghero has a large port which allows even sizeable boats safe docking. The countryside is well known for its olive groves and vineyards, while the shoreline has an array of small bays, creeks, reefs, and beaches. The area is just right for enjoying many water sports such as fishing, swimming, windsurfing, sailing, and scuba diving. The *Grotte di Netttuno* can be reached by sea, or land by way of the *Escala del Cabirol*, nearly six hundred and fifty cliffside steps that lead into this cavernous area. We rented a small motorboat for the day, which was a delightful way to appreciate much of what this *Coral Riviera* has to offer.

Club Hotel Li Capanni

Director: Gianluca Innocenti
Via Lungomare, 07020 / Cannigione, Italy
Telephone: ++ 39 0789 86041 / Fax: ++39 0789 86200
E-mail: licapanni@tiscali.it / Website: www.licapanni.com

★★★ **Price guide:** Rent your own Sardinian hotel with private cottages from €45,000–€60,000/per week/44 maximum people/all meals inclusive/drinks not included • Major credit cards accepted • Nearest airport: Olbia • Nearest harbors: Olbia and Golfo Arancia • Nearest towns: Baia Sardinia, Cannigione **Amenities:** Babysitting • Bar • Laundry • Parking • Private Beach • Restaurant/personal chef **Activities:** Available by previous arrangement; Boating • Do-In (Oriental breathing classes) • Fishing • Sailing • Scuba Diving • Snorkeling • Kayaking • Yoga • Excursions to nearby islands, vineyards, and archaeological sites **Additional Information:** Prior to arrival, create your dream holiday by personalizing your week with your favorite activities, events and menu suggestions • Drivers and rental cars can be arranged • Property best suited for large families, and corporate conventions

Li Capanni is set amid twelve acres with some of Sardinia's most beautiful and unscathed scenery. Twenty rustic terracotta cottages are strategically positioned at the summit of the property overlooking the private beach with an extensive sea view. Li Capanni can comfortably house thirty to forty people. An inclusive week stay includes three meals daily of delicious homemade Mediterranean food prepared by your personal chef from the neighboring island of Maddalena. Typical Sardinian cuisine, which includes fresh local seafood, produce, cheese, and wine combined with a spectacular panoramic view of the sea, makes dinning a special experience. The accommodations are simple and authentic, containing only the bare essential such as beds, tables, chairs, wardrobes, and nightstands. Each dwelling has its own bathroom with shower. Having what is necessary for a comfortable stay freed us from the immensities of our everyday life. Surrounded by the calm murmurs of the sea along with eye-catching flora emitting exotic aromas, soothed our souls while calming our minds.

The director, Gianluca and his wife Brit, were constantly on hand catering to our needs. Together they continually balance the requirements of both their young son Niklas and the organization of running the hotel. Gianluca says, "At Li Capanni you are only limited by your imagination. We are here to make your fantasies into a reality." This is your own Sardinian hotel for a week, regardless of the number of people, with the maximum being forty-four. Anything you want, they will arrange to make this the unique holiday experience you have anticipated. Nothing is too much: a romantic dinner on the beach with your own personal display of fireworks or sail away on a private yacht to the nearby islands. Gianluca and his staff organized an exclusive dinner in honor of my birthday. The Barroni family, natives of the Lombardy region of Italy and our neighbors in Atlanta, joined us for my celebration. Our feast was served on the terrace overlooking the sea in the midst of a magnificent sunset. A seemingly endless flow of food was continually served, beginning with tender *calamari* in a delectable wine sauce, through to the finale of a freshly baked caked.

Li Capanni will plan local excursions, to vineyards, archaeological sites, as well as a children's water park. Nevertheless, sunbathing, snorkeling, and swimming on our private beach in one of Europe's best locations was simply divine.

David cruising Europe's canals aboard a Crown Blue Line *boat*

Boats, Skiing, Villas & More

Crown Blue Line

United States Office:
General Manager: Peter Cook / Vacation coordinator: Jill Harner
Annapolis Landing Marina / 980 Awald Road / Suite 302 / Annapolis, Maryland USA / 21403
Telephone: 888-355-9491 or 800-355-9394 / Fax: 410-280-2406
E-Mail: crownbluelineus@att.net / Web: www.crownblueline.com

United Kingdom Office:
Vacation Coordinator: Jessica Thurlow
The Port House / Port Solent Portsmouth / Hampshire, United Kingdom / PO6 4TH
Telephone: ++44 870 240 8393 / Fax: ++44 870 770 6301
E-Mail: boating@crownblueline.co.uk

When your pace of life is moving at the speed of a Concorde jet, slow down and take hold of the wheel onboard a Crown Blue Line boat. Watch the world go by as you cruise the canals and rivers of Europe. Your bikes on board await their use as you dock and explore a nearby village or vineyard.

Crown Blue Line offers sixteen cruising regions. Choose excursions through France, Germany, Holland, Ireland, and of course, Italy. Desiring to give Jacob an extended opportunity to practice his French while having a different cultural experience for all, we choose the Canal du Midi. This is the oldest artificial waterway in Europe; moreover, it's designed by Paul Riquet and links the Aquitaine with the Mediterranean. This entry point enabled us to begin our journey in the heart of France,

depositing us at the mouth of the Mediterranean, the perfect location for entry to the French Riviera and on to the Italian coast. For more than thirty years, Crown Blue Line has been providing quality boating vacations throughout Europe.

Prior to leaving the United States, we received manuals that explained the details of our soon-to-be sojourn. At our departure point in Castelnaudary, France, friendly and professional bilingual staff was present to ensure our safety. We were escorted to our boat, the Classique, where we had hands-on operating instructions. However, nothing can prepare you for the thrill and exhilaration of maneuvering your first lock. Most locks on the Canal du Midi are still manually operated with a lock keeper present. This is a real art, which takes some strength and diligence; however, the boats are easy to handle and require no driver's license.

What I most enjoyed was the uninterrupted moments we had as a family, with no television or radio to drown out conversations. We all worked together - well the boys would argue that point with me. They all worked collectively as a team to get us through the many locks, two ashore, one at the wheel. Ropes to be tied around the bollards holding tight, while another one handles the sluice gates. Me? Well, you know, someone has to prepare the meals!

One of the funniest moments occurred as we were cruising along. Ari, at the interior steering position, had proved his competency early on after many successful lock maneuvers. Isaac was in the bathroom as David, Jake, and I were on the upper sun deck, feasting on bread, cheese, fruit, and wine under the parasol. Relaxed and peaceful, we were oblivious that the boat was heading inadvertently toward shore. Ari had abandoned the wheel after announcing to Isaac, Take over, I'm going up!" Within seconds, we had mayhem onboard. As I yelled, "Hit the deck!" we each grabbed what we could of our lunch along with the chairs, table, and parasol, diving face down to avoid concussions by overhanging trees. Truly, Isaac must have gotten the worst end of the stick!

As we journeyed along the canal, we had many unexpected discoveries: a chateau in the distance, small villages with open street markets of food, linen and clothes, and a private vineyard Ari and I discovered on a bike ride. We purchased two bottles of wine that were extracted directly from the vat into the bottles and corked before our eyes. Total cost was $3.50. The $2.00 red was more expensive than the white.

After passing through numerous locks, we came upon the old city of Carcassone, known for having the largest fortress in Europe. However, what my boys will always associate this splendid old city with are their Belgium waffles and crepes covered with strawberry preserves and *nutella*

(chocolate hazelnut spread), then piled high with fresh, whipped cream! They devoured them for dinner and breakfast the following morning.

Crown Blue Line offers a unique experience to see Venice by boat. There are an abundance of waterways to romance you through this city. Visit the islands of Murano, Burano, and Torcello, or visit the picturesque beaches of Lido and Bibione. They have a suggested itinerary of one week. Many of their trips can be broken down into shorter excursions. These shorter breaks are available at certain periods such as mid-week and weekends. Prices are available upon request.

There are thirty-seven different types of boats and three class distinctions from which to choose. We recommend their Crown Class boats that offer a little more luxury. The boat we chose was the Classique. Although the description indicates it sleeps eight, we found the space just ample for our family of five. The most luxurious in the Classique range is the Royal Classique. Its spaciousness, air-conditioning, and microwave oven is worth the upgrade. It sleeps six but is much roomier. If you plan to travel with extended family or friends, for added comfort and privacy, rent individual boats. It is quite easy to stay close together as you float down the canals in unison.

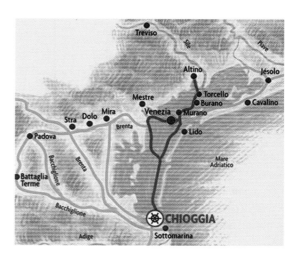

Scuola Sci Cortina

Dolomite Ski School
Chairperson: Mauro Ponti / Manager: Franco Siorpaes
Corso Italia / Ciasa de ra Regoles / 32043 Cortina d'Ampezzo (BL)
Telephone: +39 0436 2911 / Fax: +39 0436 3495
E-mail: info@scuolascicortina.it / Web: www.scuolascicortina.com

As the sun rises over the Dolomites, the mountains reflect a pinkish hue, reminiscent of the coral from the old seabed. Cortina is an international resort that hosts many world cup events such as the 1956 Olympics and is home to "Scuola Sci Cortina." Franco, the Director, has a charisma and passion that captured me from the start. His eagerness to inform us about the one hundred ski trails and famous Dolomite Super Ski area, which provide 1,207 kilometers of skiing for all levels, was contagious. Scuola Sci Cortina is positioned in the central part of Cortina next to the famous large clock tower; however, to purchase your ski lift tickets, head for the Ufficio Skipass Office located in town on Via Marconi next to the polizia municipale.

Scuola Sci Cortina's professional staff of 120 top-notch instructors are warm and friendly; furthermore, most are multilingual. Mauro, the President, and Franco, are always nearby to acquaint you with their 100 year-old tradition of being Italy's premier winter resort. The Dolomite mountains and Scuola Sci Cortina offer unlimited and endless skiing with the most dramatic snow-covered pistas (slopes) of the Dolomites. Their first class attentive teachers are specialists in either skiing or snowboarding, and are eager to facilitate your family in enjoying the sport while transmitting their skill and knowledge. Isaac and Ari were initially hesitant at the prospect of a foreign instructor; however, the teachers are accustomed to dealing with language diversity. Jacob's inherent love of linguistics was further nourished as was his skiing competency. Isaac and Ari emerged with measurable improvement on the slopes and additional familiarity of the Italian language. Giving your kids the exposure to diverse cultures unlocks their intelligence to better perceive the immenseness of our world.

David and I escorted the boys each morning, placing them into the hands of their maestros (teachers). Together we delighted in a casual yet challenging alpine experience. The attitude on the mountain in Italy is much more laid back in comparison to the United States. By 1:00 p.m. when the runs are virtually empty, family and food take precedence. Some of the finest cuisine available is located directly on the mountain, accessible by car, skis, or snowboard. David, the

boys, and I would rendezvous at noon after ski school. The terrace patio of the restaurant presented spectacular views and unforgettable casunziei (ravioli with beets topped with a sage butter sauce) and more. The restaurant, at the base adjacent to the parking lot, served a more basic fare. Italian families gather slope-side in the afternoon relaxing in lounge chairs equipped with picnic baskets, sun reflectors, carriages, sleds, pails, and shovels. Many, dressed to the hilt in mink coats, appear regal and beautiful. This continues until the warmth of the sun disappears. Our afternoons were less hurried contrasted to life in the U.S., but we always returned to ski and snowboard with the boys. They loved showing us their progress, and we enjoyed the daily camaraderie by skiing down the mountain together as they surpassed our own abilities. There is no doubt why Scuola Sci Cortina has remained the largest and best ski school in all of Italy.

Scinsieme

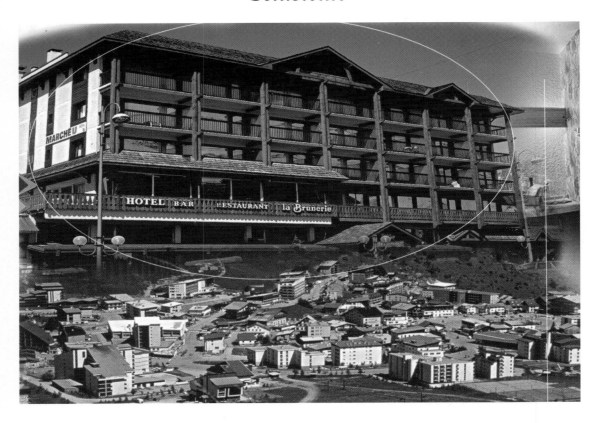

A summer ski & snowboard camp
Directors: Giovanni Migliardi, Renato Rosci, Massimo Debernardi
Marketing Director: Massimo Pastorino
Cellular Tel: ++39 348 4448093
Corso Liberta' 8 / 14053 Canelli (AT) / Italy
Tel: 0141 82 3985 / Fax: 0141 82 2380
&
Hotel La Brunerie / Les Deux Alpes
Tel: ++33 476 79 2223 / Fax: ++33 476 79 5733
E- mail: scinsieme@virgilio.it / Web: www.scinsieme.com

For all those who can't get enough skiing and snowboarding in the winter, the resort of Les Deux Alpes is situated in the French Alps, less than two hours from Torino, Italy. The camp offers 2,575 vertical feet of glacier skiing and snowboarding on more than 200 *hecters* (.40 = 1 acre) of snow in the summer! The area even has an underground funicular Dome Express to transport you up to the mountain summit. With over 35,000 quest beds, more than 200 shops and 40 restaurants, *Les 2 Alpes* is one of the liveliest resorts in the Alps. Nightclubs stay open until dawn, although Scinsieme has strict rules for their under-age campers.

One or two week sessions from June through September provide kids with immense fun both on and off the slopes. All campers stay at Hotel La Brunerie, located in the center of *Les 2 Alpes*, which is owned and operated by the camp. The directors and instructors all reside at the hotel giving continual supervision with very little spare time. However, you may appreciate spending the week at the hotel with the kids while they are engaged in an organized program of activities. My friend Daniela Borroni did just that with her ten-year-old son, Edward, enabling her to have ample personal time both on and off the slopes. During their stay, the 2002 Tour de France spent a number of race days in the Alps and came directly into *Les 2 Alpes* creating excitement and a great party atmosphere.

As a family, we had been traveling throughout Italy for four weeks; therefore, our kids were so excited at the idea of being on their own for one

week. David and I stayed the first night wanting to wish Isaac a happy thirteenth birthday the next morning, then set off on a journey of our own. We spent the night at the home of our friends from Atlanta in their rustic, peaceful chalet on top of the French Alps. On their recommendation, we traveled on to the romantic medieval village and resort of Peruge, followed by a few magical nights in Paris and Lyon.

After arrival and check-in, an all-camp preliminary meeting is held to familiarize the kids with the rules and each other. They are placed in groups and assigned a counselor for the week who is also their ski or snowboard instructor. The directors are keen on placing the kids according to their ability level and language needs.

The daily schedule at Scinsieme begins with breakfast at 7:00 a.m. followed by ski school from 8:00 a.m. until 12:00 p.m., when the glacier begins to melt by this point in the day and the mountain closes. Lunch is served at 1:30 p.m. Activities begin again at 3:30 p.m., and your kids get to choose between swimming, tennis, archery, bobsled, golf, mountain bike, bungee jumping, trampoline, four-wheeling, paintball, para-sailing, or soccer. Dinner is usually between 6:00 p.m. and 8:00 p.m., depending on the finishing point of the afternoon events. Following dinner, the groups meet and go bowling, ice-skating, shopping, listen to local music groups, or even ride a mechanical rodeo bull. The last night is an awards and talent show for the entire camp. My boys teamed up with a group of Italian kids and they taught the American national anthem and, in turn, they learned the Italian national anthem, resulting in a comical performance by all.

Our kids loved the unique opportunity to ski and snowboard in the warmer summer months; however, each left having cherished something different. Ari favored going out with his group to eat French *crepes* (pancakes) covered with *Nutella* (chocolate hazelnut spread), strawberry jam and whipped cream. Isaac took pleasure in the extreme challenge of the terrain course with half-pipe for snowboarding, while Jacob appreciated the nice group of kids and has maintained contact with a few.

One taste of chef Bisetti's food at Hotel La Brunerie and you'll recognize that you are at an authentic Italian resort in the French Alps. To quote the kids: "It has outstanding food with plenty of pasta accompanied by different meats, fish, vegetables, and pastries. They served everything and lots of it!" Should your kids still be hungry, the hotel bar continually serves light snacks with hot and cold drinks. Prior to leaving your kids, you can pre-pay for additional items they may consume during the week.

Aside from Hotel La Brunerie's restaurant and bar, it has a sauna, swimming pool, spa, billiards, and arcade, as well as 58 tidy dormitory-style rooms each with its own bathroom, telephone and television.

Hotel La Brunerie's cost without skiing or snowboarding is:

- €365-€480 plus tax, per person for one week which includes:
- Six days full *pension* (bed, breakfast, lunch, & dinner)
- Organized activities

Discounts:

- Kids 3-8 less €130
- 3rd adult in same room less €50
- 4th adult in same room less €100
- Half pension (only bed & breakfast with lunch or dinner) less €7/day
- 2 consecutive weeks less €50
- 2 adults & 2 kids 10 and under = cost of 3 adults

Supplement:
- Single room €77
- Kids 0-3 years €15/ day

6 day lift pass:
- Adult €137
- Kids thirteen years and under €110

Scinsieme camp cost:
- 7-day session: €653
Includes:
- Complete *Pension* (bed, breakfast, lunch & dinner)
- 6-day ski/snowboard pass
- 6-day ski/snowboard school
- 2 video tapings on slope
- Ski race & awards ceremony
- Organized afternoon activities
- Tax

14-day session:
- €1120
Includes:
- Complete *Pension* (bed, breakfast, lunch & dinner)
- 12-day ski/snowboard pass
- 10-day ski/snowboard school
- 4 video tapings on slope
- Ski race & awards ceremony
- Organized afternoon activities
- Tax

Language courses:
- €50 week
- Two hours a day
Most Credit cards excepted
Non-refundable deposit required/€130

Tuscany Now

Villa Rentals & More...
Owner: Simon and Barbara Ball
10/18 Vestry Street / London N1 7RE / England
Telephone: ++4402076848884 / Fax: ++4402076848880
E-Mail: accounts@tuscanynow.com
sales@tuscanynow.com / brochure@tuscanynow.com
Web: www.tuscanynow.com

Go to the internet, search *Villas in Italy*, and a myriad of possibilities will avail themselves to you, many reputable, and most lacking knowledge and experience in an industry that requires extensive awareness of the country and its culture.

Simon and Barbara Ball developed *TuscanyNow* over twelve years ago. Their roots grow deep in Italy for Simon grew up on a farm in the hills south of Florence, and Barbara is a Florentine native. In their humble beginnings, they developed marketing strategies to promote the family's home and that of two friends. Their goal was to produce ample income to support the overhead and maintenance of these abodes. They now offer more than 150 properties in the region of Calabra, Campania, Emilia, Lazio, Marche, Sicily, Tuscany, Umbria, and Veneto along with the islands of Capri, Maratea, Panarea, Pantelleria, Sardegna, and Vulcano. One glance at their brochure will assure you that *TuscanyNow* is a first rate company.

Simon, Barbara, and their accommodating indigenous Italian staff are passionate about helping to choose a suitable accommodation for your family. Their first criterion for booking a property is a phone interview to establish your exact needs. Simon steered me away from a few properties that he felt were not satisfactory for our children and our particular requirements. Simon and Barbara are anxious to share their Italy with you; moreover, *TuscanyNow* will design the ideal home away from home holiday for your family.

TuscanyNow's recommendation of Villa Pozzarello, located ten minutes from my favorite Umbrian town of Orvieto, was *fantastico*! Breakfast on the loggia overlooking the swimming pool while facing the gothic Duomo of Orvieto was only the beginning. The original stone farmhouse was remodeled and transformed into an up-to-date grandiose holiday home that can accommodate up to fourteen people. The villa is aesthetically furnished to equal its imposing surroundings yet homey and comfortable for a relaxed *TuscanyNow* experience. Amazing views of the Umbrian countryside surrounded us amidst our private vineyard, tennis court, and adjacent guesthouse.

There was so much to see and experience at our back door. Besides the Duomo with paintings by Beato Angelico, Luca Signorelli, Lippo Memmi and Gentile da Fabriano, visit the Papal Palaces, the 13th century Palazzo del Popolo, and numerous archeological sites and vast churches. My sister-in-law, Helene, and I spent several hours roaming the boutiques and shops for *ceramiche* (ceramics). Particularly, near the Duomo, we were impressed with the quality of pottery and craftsmanship available. "Ceramiche Giacomini" in Piazza Duomo was some of the finest in the area. The position of our villa enabled us to make excursions to other Umbrian towns of Gubbio and Todi. When the children were well rested, fed, and exercised, we ventured as far as Arezzo, Florence, and Pitigliano, also known as "little Jerusalem."

On some days, we were content to remain at the Pozzarello, lingering at the pool and on the tennis court.

Umbrian cuisine is distinctive with earthy characteristic quality. For an authentic taste, try Restaurant dell'Ancora located on Via de Piazza del Popolo, telephone ++390763342766. David's brother and sister-in-law, Pete and Helene, joined us in celebrating our nineteenth wedding anniversary at La Badia down the road from Pozzarello. It is a castle converted into a hotel and restaurant. The food and service were first rate. My boys, niece Laurin, and nephew Jason, remained at the villa exhausted from the day's non-stop swimming.

TuscanyNow is well aligned with other businesses that can simplify your traveling concerns. *European Travel* will arrange flights, hotels, and car rentals. *La Baccanti* are specialists in setting up luxury custom tours of vineyards, cooking classes and shopping. They offer the services of a company that provides quality chauffeur driven cars. Mattisse is a cordon bleu chef who can provide outstanding meals in many of the villas in Tuscany. Most of the properties have maids who are capable of preparing lunches and dinners. If you desire food shopping done in advance of your arrival, fill out the "extra services form" while completing your registration. Should you agree with Simon, Barbara, and I that Italy is the most beautiful country in the world, you may want to speak with T. N. Real Estate Ltd. to purchase your ideal property.

Tuscan Sunflower Field

Reservation Request

LEVINSON TRAVEL GUIDES
www.levinsontravel.com

Date: _____   ATTENTION: Reservation Manager

Hotel Name: _____
Telephone:_____ FAX: _____ E-MAIL:_____

Our Surname: _____
First Name: _____
Street Address: _____
City:_____ State: _____ Zip: _____ Country: _____
Telephone: _____ FAX: _____ E-MAIL_____

Arrival Date: _____ Departure Date: _____
Total Number of Guests: _____ Adults: _____ Children: _____
AGES: Child #1: _____ Child #2: _____ Child #3: _____ Child #4: _____

ACCOMMODATION: We Desire
#_____ Single Room #_____ Double Room #_____Connecting Rooms
#_____ Junior Suite #_____ Superior Suite

FOOD PLAN: ❑ Bed & Breakfast   ❑ Half-Board ❑ Full-Board

PLEASE QUOTE IN: ❑ Euro   ❑ USD   ❑ Other

HOTEL: PLEASE SEND US THE FOLLOWING INFORMATION:
Confirmation of Availability: Dates _____ Number of Rooms_____
Type of Room _____ Food Plan _____

TOTAL COST: _____ Deposit Required: _____ Refund Policy: _____

CREDIT CARDS EXCEPTED: ❑ VISA   ❑ MC   ❑ AMEX   ❑ OTHER

MY FINAL CONFIRMATION: We will arrive: _____ and depart: _____
Credit Card: _____ Card Number: _____ Expiration Date: _____
Deposit Amount: _____ Signature: _____

Please print this form and fax it to the properties to make your reservation requests.
You may also download this form on line at: www.levinsontravel.com
Levinson Travel Guides © Copyright 2003

Today **Go-Ped** is the global leader in motorized scooter sales, and is an established brand among extreme sports enthusiast. *Go-Peds* are also growing in popularity as an alternative transport vehicle for city dwellers with short or disconnected commutes.

We had the best time riding our *Go-Peds* through the streets of Italy, especially some of the smaller medieval towns such as Orvieto, Arezzo and Sorento.

Thanks Patmont Motor Werks,
Jacob, Isaac & Ari Levinson

150 Countries Worldwide, One Number
Phone Number Before Departure
Lowest Rates Guaranteed
Shipped Overnight

TravelCell made it possible for us to stay in touch with family, friends, & colleagues throughout Italy. Identify yourself as a Levinson Traveler and receive a discount off the basic rental fee.

Around The World, Anytime!
Call 1-877-CELL-PHONE
Or www.travelcell.com

Frequent Flyer: Livio Panebianco

Quality wines don't come knocking on your front door.... finding them is the trick.

PANEBIANCO
Selections

1140 Broadway Suite 504 New York 10001, NY 212 685 7560   email: wines@panebiancollc.com

O N E

LEADING HOTELS PRESENTS

MORE

THE ULTIMATE LATE CHECK - OUT

NIGHT

FOR A LIMITED TIME, GUESTS WHO BOOK THREE NIGHTS AT A PARTICIPATING LEADING HOTEL WILL RECEIVE A COMPLIMENTARY FOURTH NIGHT. It's one more night to propose a toast, one more night to hear the locals sing and just one more reason to choose a Leading Hotel for the perfect trip. For reservations, information or to receive your complimentary Leading Hotels of the World 2003 Directory, please contact your travel professional or Leading Hotels or visit www.lhw.com/one.

The Leading Hotels of the World®

00800 30 40 60 70 / 1800 223 6800
WWW.LHW.COM/ONE

Rates subject to availability, some restrictions may apply.

Travel Log